Logistics - The Transport and Distribution Aspects
a text for all interested in this subject

Noel A. McInerney

An Foras um Cheannacht agus Bainistíocht Ábhar
Irish Institute of Purchasing and Materials Management

Published by the Irish Institute of Purchasing and Materials Management
An Foras um Cheannacht agus Bainistíocht Ábhar
5 Belvedere Place
Dublin 1.
Republic of Ireland

First Published 1997
(as Logistics - Transport and Distribution)
Second Edition 1998
Logistics- The Transport and Distribution Aspects

Reprinted October 1999

British Library Cataloguing in Publication Data
A CIP record for this book is available from the British Library
ISBN 0 9534335 0 1

Typeset and Printed in the Republic of Ireland

My Sincere Thanks to Julia Malone R.I.P., JM(2) and P Pio. Noel

Preface

Logistics -
The Transport and Distribution Aspects

Logistics is concerned with the integrated management of *Buying, Stockholding, Transport,* and *Distribution*. It is a fundamental principle of logistics that these areas of business and other related activities, *e.g. Materials control and Production planning*, should be closely co-ordinated.
Because the term "*Logistics*" is used incorrectly by sections of the business community, in a narrow sense to describe movement of materials or transportation alone, some readers may be surprised to learn that the term covers much more.

This text is concerned with assisting *all* students of *Logistics* to acquire a useful knowledge and a valuable understanding of two Logistics aspects, *Transport and Distribution*. The comprehensive section on *Distribution* will give students the opportunity of learning this subject from *concept to implementation*. The *Transport* section covers what is involved in the choice and use of *Transport*, both to bring materials into a company and to ship materials out of a company.

Students of the IIPMM *first-year certificate course*, will see references to *"Logistics"* in three of the four subjects on the course.
It is important, therefore, to read carefully the first section of this text - "*Introduction to Logistics*" to appreciate why the management roles of *Purchasing and of Stores Control* are intrinsic to the overall *Logistics* function of any company.
This will explain why students will notice an element of overlap in the subjects; although the IIPMM syllabus has been designed to keep this to a minimum.

We wish our IIPMM students, and all students, every success in their studies and in their examinations; and we look forward to hearing of continued successes in both their business and private lives.

IIPMM Education Committee 1998-2000

Remember YOUR name can be on this!

Attend your classes regularly, study systematically and your name WILL be on this.

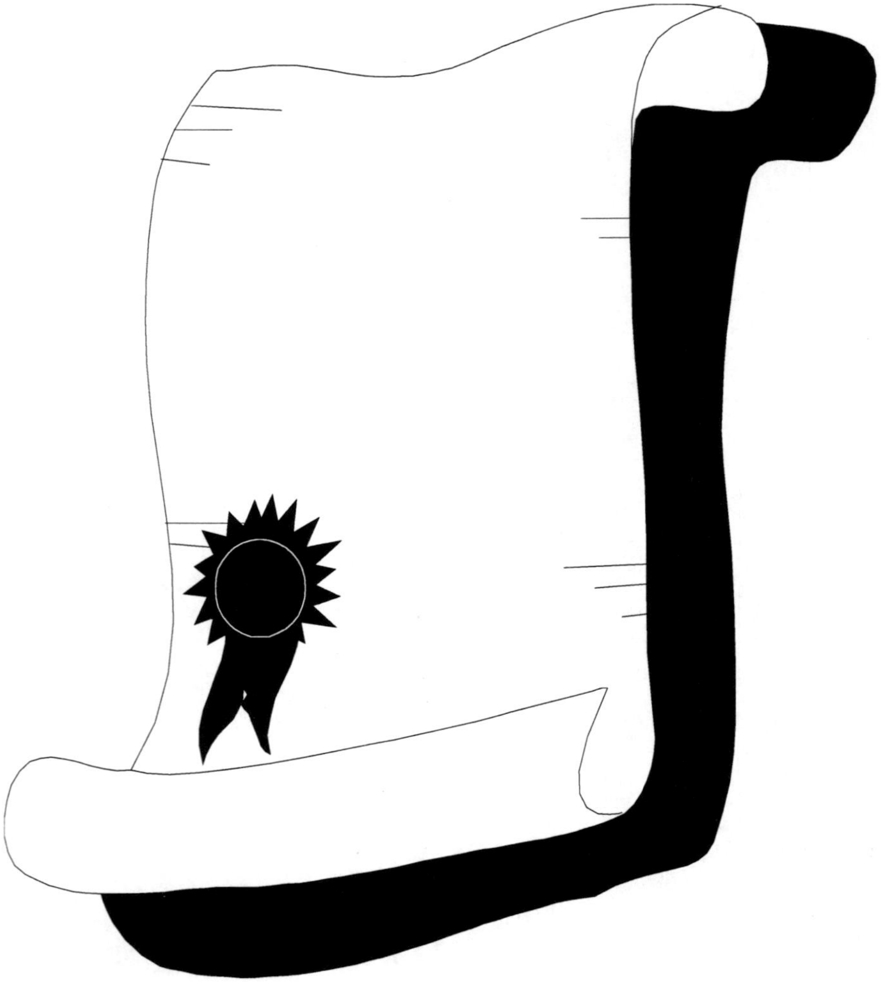

Contents

Contents continued

Contents continued

Contents continued

Contents continued

Quick-Find Chapter Titles

Part One: Logistics of Packaging, Handling, Storing and Transporting the Product

1 Four Important Definitions:

Logistics - Materials Management:

Materials Management is the total of all those tasks, functions, activities, and routines that concern the transfer of external materials and services into the organization, and the administration of the same until they are consumed or used in the process of production, operations or sale.

Logistics - Distribution Concept:

Distribution is a system or network of channels, chosen by an organization to enable its finished goods (or services), to be made available to the market or markets of its choice.

Logistics - Physical Distribution Management:

Physical Distribution Management (PDM), is the task of ensuring that the goods, or services, produced by an organization are transported from the place of production, or origination, to the point of consumption, as safely, efficiently, and as economically as possible. This involves keeping the total stock, transportation and storage costs as low as possible.

Logistics - Transport:

Transport is the means or process by which people and goods are moved from one location to another, safely, conveniently, and as economically as possible.
Goods must be moved to a point of Distribution in order to be made available to the ultimate consumer..

2 Introduction to Logistics

The term Logistics has produced different definitions from different authors, depending on their bias towards Marketing, Production, or Distribution. Institutions have changed their definition of Logistics to accomodate additional activities regarded as "logistical".
The definitive description of Logistics still has to be composed.

The origin of the word comes from the French - *lager* meaning *to lodge or quarter.* The term has its origin in describing the movement and accommodation of materials and personnel involved in *Military* operations; e.g. the work of a quartermaster.
To list out the various definitions of Logistics at the beginning, would confuse rather than inform, any student new to this subject. We shall look at a current basic definition of Logistics; and develop our understanding from there.

"Logistics is the strategic management of the total supply chain".

By looking at the "Supply-Chain" chart, one immediately can appreciate the many activites involved in Logistics. Later we shall call details of these, the "Activity Mix".

American authors Dobler, Burt & Lee in the 1991 edition of their respected text "Purchasing and Materials Management" define Logistics as the combination of the activities of:
"Materials Management (MM) plus Physical Distribution Management (PDM)"

This can be used as a basis; from which to work up to a comprehensive description of Logistics; one that is accepted by most business organizations today. We shall begin by looking at the various activities of MM and PDM, the ***Logistics Activity Mix.***

Where does Materials Management end, and PDM begin?

(a) Materials Management incorporates the total flow of information and materials into the organization ending at the production line
(b) Physical Distribution Management refers to the flow of materials from the production line to the end user. It supports the marketing concept of *customer service.*

Logistics -- Supply-Chain Elements

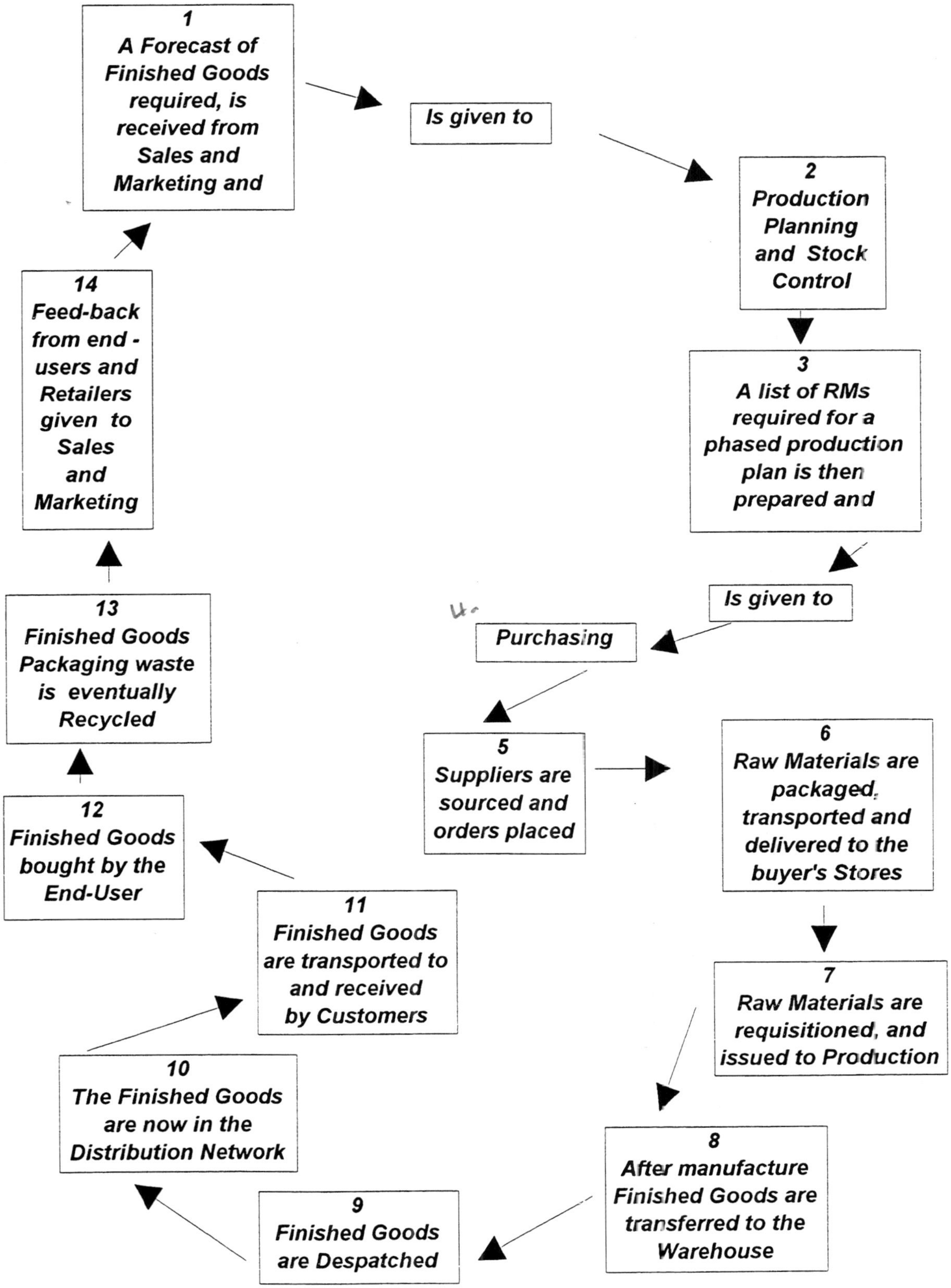

The Logistics "Activity-Mix"

Materials Management (MM)

What is Materials Management?

"Materials Management is the total of all those tasks, functions, activities, and routines that concern the transfer of external materials and services into the organization, and the administration of the same until they are consumed or used in the process of production, operations or sale."

<u>Analysing the above definition, shows that MM is concerned with the following:</u>

(1) Stores and Warehousing.
(2) Safety and Security issues.
(3) Information Management.
(4) Raw Materials Inventory Management.
(Stock-Control, Stock-Takes)
(5) Production-Planning, Scheduling and Control.
(6) Procurement Activities.
(Sourcing, Buying, Negotiating, Value Analysis
(7) Protective Packaging.
(8) Choice of Transport mode
(9) Transportation of items into the company.
(Raw Materials, Machine or Maintenance parts)
(10) Customs Clearance
(11) Receiving Activities.
(Goods-Inward Procedures)
(12) In-plant Materials Handling
(13) Packaging-Waste Management.
(14) Surplus / Salvage.
(Disposal of materials or seeking alternate uses)

Physical Distribution Management (PDM)

What is meant by PDM?

PDM is best understood by describing its Primary and Secondary tasks.
The Primary task of PDM is the consideration, the co-ordination, and the integration of the distribution responsibilities of all other departments; which are engaged in different aspects of distribution.
The initial PDM decisions involve:
(a) Determination of the CSL - Customer Service Level, i.e. deciding the "ideal" quantities to be kept in stock. CSL calculation: the number of customer orders available ex stock expressed as a percentage of the total orders received in the same period.
Compare desired CSL with the actual position, and
(b) Agree appropiate Stock Levels to be held by the company.
The Secondary task of PDM is one of ensuring that the finished goods or services produced by the organization are transported from the Production point to the Consumption point, as efficiently and as economically as possible.

<u>Fulfilling its tasks, involves PDM in consideration of the following:</u>

(1) Warehousing.
(2) Safety and Security issues.
(3) Finished goods.
(4) Packaging (e.g. identification and ease of handling in safety)
(5) Sales Order processing. Includes convenience for customers in placing order(s) and advising on availability
(6) Movement / Transportation of Goods
(7) Customer Service. Includes "point of sale" support.
(8) Information Management.
(9) Finished Goods Inventory Maintenance.
(Setting of Customer Service Levels)
(10) Selection / Marshalling / Loading goods
(11) Shipment Frequency.
(12) Choice of Transport mode. (e.g. Sea or Air)
(13) Despatch. Includes suitability of documentation and reliability of delivery.
(14) Packaging-Waste Management.

Introduction to Logistics (continued)

At this point a couple of simple definitions of MM and PDM should help students new to this subject.

> *Materials Management* incorporates the total flow of information and materials into the organization *ending at the production line*.
>
> *Physical Distribution Management* refers to the flow of materials *from the production line* to the end user. It supports the marketing concept of customer service.

Both the Society of Logistics Engineers (SOLE) in the US, and the Institute of Logistics (formerly the Institute of Logistics and Distribution Management) in the UK, have used the following definitions of Logistics:

> *"Logistics is the process of managing the movement and storage of goods and materials from their source to the point of ultimate consumption"*
>
> *"Logistics is the time related positioning of resources or, the strategic management of the total supply chain"*

Logistics coverage in the IIPMM Diploma courses:
Those elements of Logistics concerning Warehousing, Stock-Control, Service Level, and Stock-Takes, are covered in the *"Stores Management & Inventory Control"* subject.

The elements of Sourcing, Value Analysis, Negotiation, and Purchasing are part of the syllabus for the subject *"Basics for Buyers"*, and the second year subject "*Purchasing Management* I".

Aspects of Production Planning and Control are discussed in both subjects; but detailed knowledge is reserved for presentation in the third year subject *"Materials and Production Planning & Control"*.

This subject **"*Transport and Distribution*",** includes coverage of the Concept of Distribution, Physical Distribution Management, Transportation into the country, within the country, out of the country, and coverage of Materials-Handling equipment.
All these activities are part of an Integrated Logistics system.

The Mission of Logistics
Logistics, although a combination of *many* activities, its mission can be stated quite simply.
The Mission of Logistics is to ensure that the correct goods get to the correct place, at the requested time, in safe and perfect condition, while making the maximum contribution to the organization's profitability.

Organization Charts

“A” Traditional Management Structure

“B” Materials Management Structure

“C” Logistics Management Structure

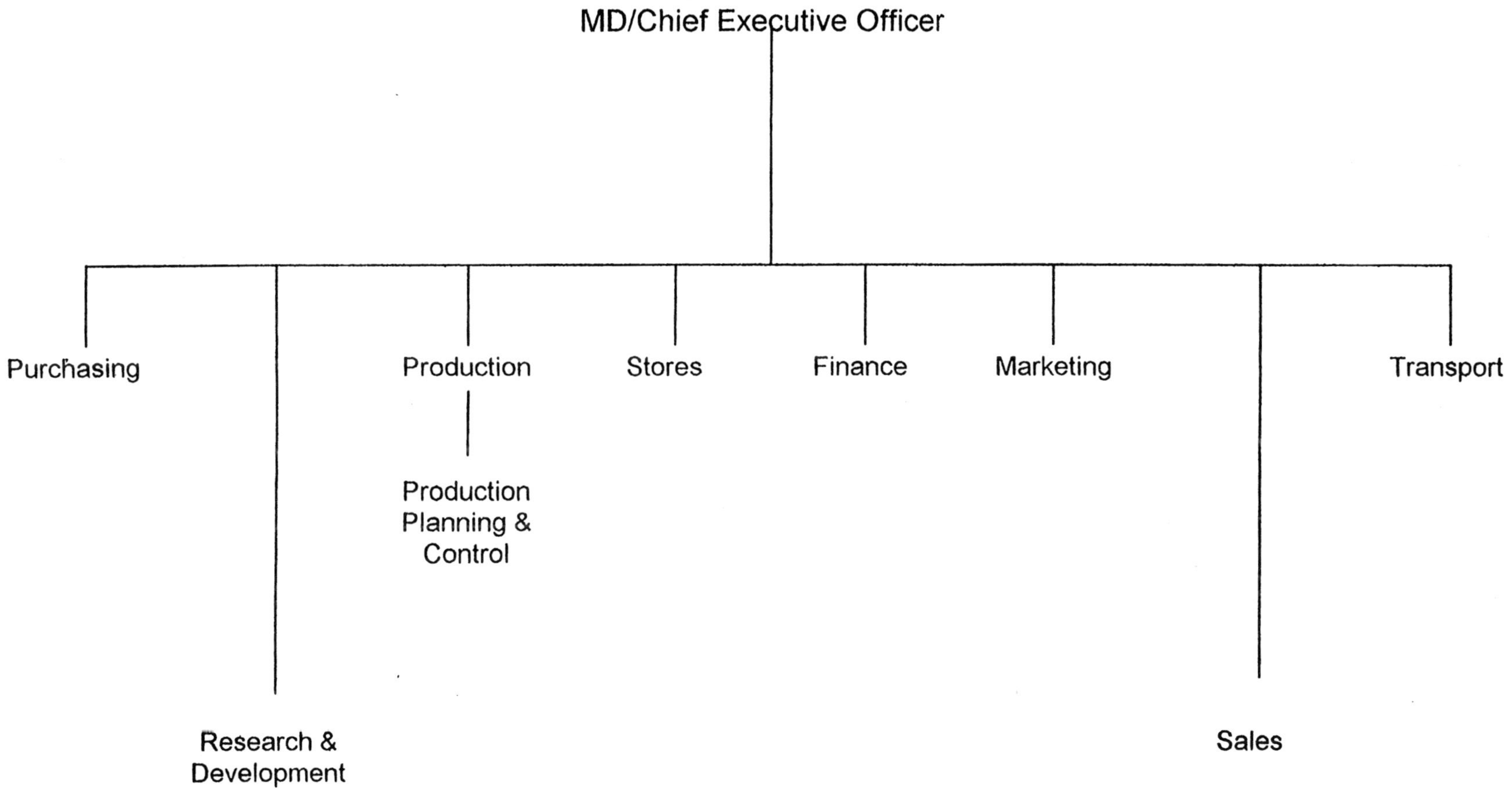

Organization Chart "A" Traditional Management Structure

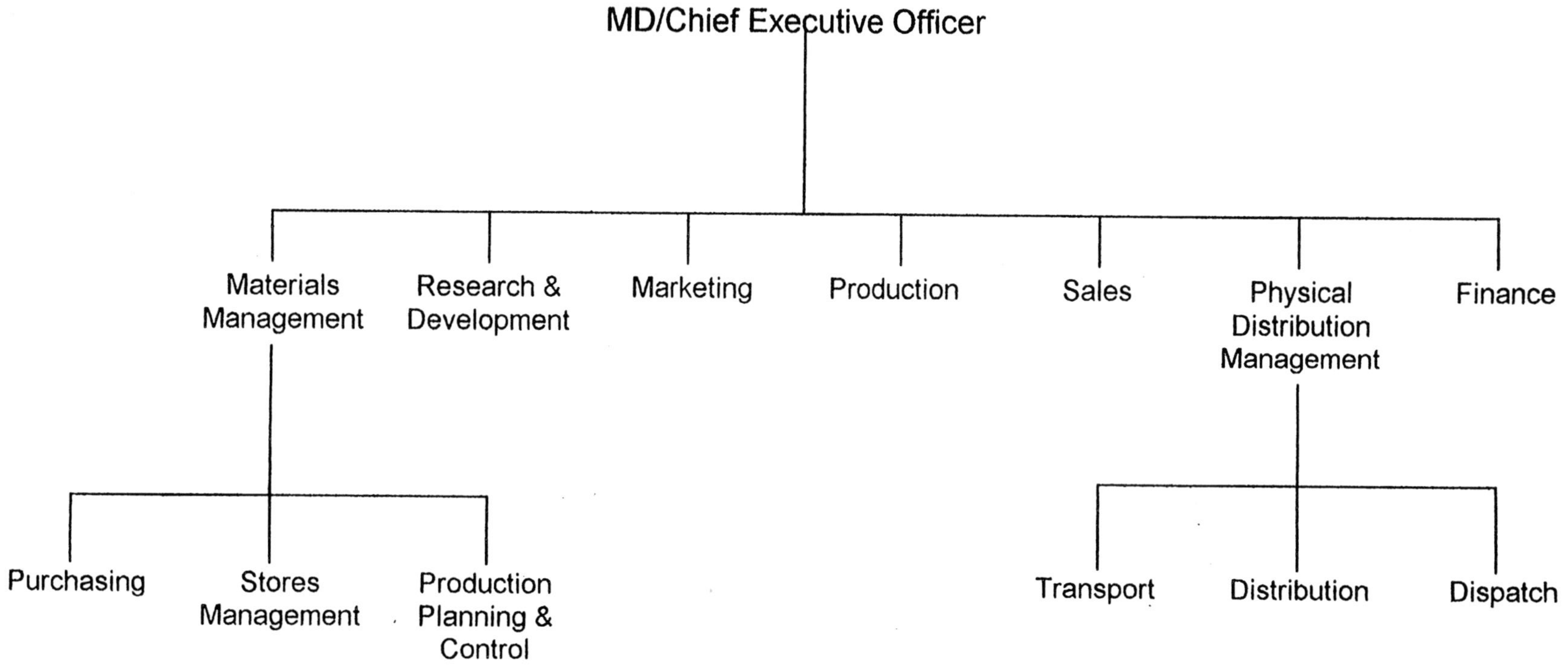

Organization Chart "B" Materials Management Structure

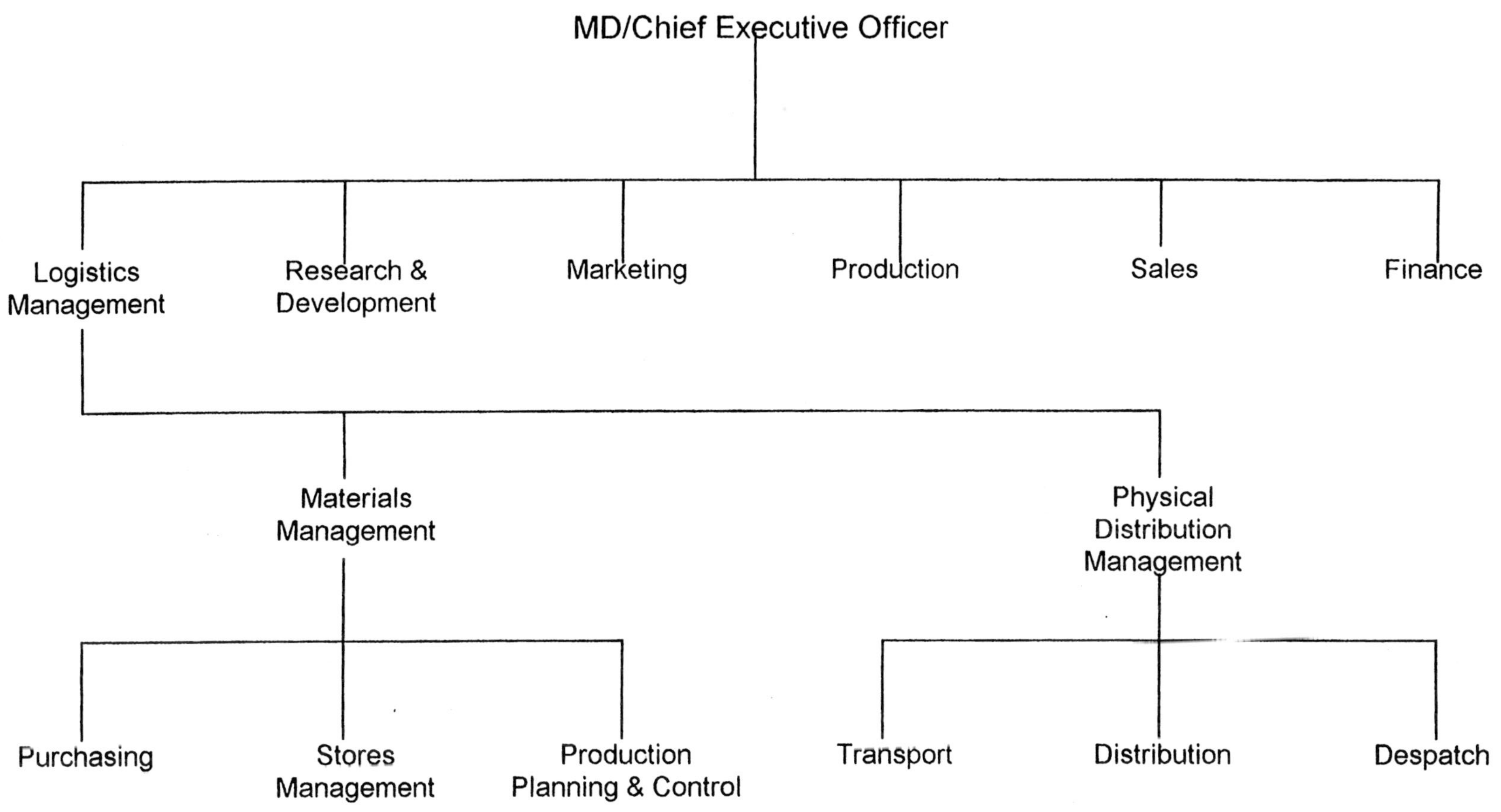

Organization Chart "C" Logistics Management Structure

The Scope of Logistics or Business Logistics

Logistics is the *combination* of the wide range of activities listed under MM and PDM.

$$L = MM + PDM$$

Business Logistics is the *concept of coordinated management of these activities*, rather than managing then separately.

These Logistics activities are continually taking place. They occur at a number of stages:
(1) mineral extraction stage (iron ore, coal, limestone),
(2) steel making stage,
(3) product production and assemble stage, and
(4) at scrap recycling stage.

The average firm has a much reduced activity list, covering only the supply of raw materials, storage and distribution of the finished product.

Advantages of Integrated Logistics

Managers and all employees in an organization are human, and they all have needs and aspirations that determine the way in which they behave. Most individuals will place their own needs above those of others. In the working environment the type of needs which people have, range from "hoping to be made permanent in one's employment", to "getting the managing director's job"!
In between these two extremes is a myriad of individual aspirations, urges and drives which individuals try to fulfil in the workplace.
There is nothing wrong in that, but often fulfilment of these *personal needs* is at the expense of the overall *company* objectives. Sometimes behaviour of this selfish type is forced on managers. Some managers who have been allocated unrealistic targets will concentrate on achieving *their* department targets in ways that could interfere with other departments' objectives.
An example of this is where a Purchasing Manager decides to buy an extra quantity of material to obtain a worthwhile quantity discount. He or she might make substantial savings for the company, and hope to become a "blue-eyed boy or girl". The reality of the situation is that the Stores Manager was probably not advised of the extra amount of materials for which he now has to find space. Most certainly, the *ignored* financial controller, will be shocked to see the eventual affect of all this on the "*cash-flow projections*." The Stock Controller will not be too pleased either! *And*, to crown it all, the extra *Cost of Storage* to cover the extra quantity purchased will, most likely, be greater than the "saving" made.

This unfortunate state of affairs, tends to happen when Stores, Transport, Purchasing, and Stock-Control report as separate departments to the Chief Executive. (See Charts). Frequently, various functions in the company strive to optimise their own set of Logistic activities, rather than those of the system as a whole.

Advantages of Integrated Logistics (continued)

The Integrated Logistics approach is one where all relevant department managers or management functions report to the one person, the Logistics Manager. This replaces the cult of the individual with one of team-work, whereby *some elements of the Logistics system operate at less than the optimum* so that the system as a whole will be more effective. Examples would be:

Production making less than economic batch sizes to reduce cost of storage, and

Transport making more frequent deliveries to give an improved service to key customers.

Benefits of this approach vary with the industry involved, but generally include the following:

Co-operation and co-ordination are promoted at the expense of unwanted conflict between departments having different objectives. *This will in time lead to less departmental "empire building."*

Improved internal and external company communications.

Morale is improved because individuals can now recognize the importance of their contribution to the overall Logistics function.

Development of inter-department respect.

More effective Purchasing and Stock Control through team-work.

Improved Transport management.

Improved customer service level as a result of smoother scheduling of requirements.

Improved company image and greater company competitiveness.

Possible Resistance to setting up a Logistics System

None of us likes to relinquish power. For example, any proposal for the setting up of Centralized Purchasing puts fear into the hearts of Buyers and Purchasing Managers. They are beset with thoughts of: will they lose power, status, even money, *or perhaps their job!*

A Logistics management structure, of its nature, requires managers to work as members of a team, not as individuals. There is a danger that *fear* expressed as stubbornness or mild aggression takes over the individual, and he may be branded straight away as being uncooperative. This is usually the case in a company not renowned for its communication skills! This type of change needs good planning.

It is a fact that when good communications *(including good feed-back)* are involved, people will co-operate with new management ideas, even those that affect themselves..

Initially, managers who have been reporting directly to the MD or CEO feel a sense of loss when they are first involved in the new Logistics management structure.

However, from working as an individual to being a team member, is a jump that appears higher than it really is. Once the fear abates, the new team player can adjust to the new situation, realizing that his job is just as important as it always was. He will notice that the other team members, for the first time perhaps, recognize the contribution he has been making to the company all along. He himself now appreciates the problems the other managers have to solve in their day-to-day work, and is prepared to co-operate with them, leaving aside all selfish interest.

3 Logistics Strategy & Planning; their place in Corporate Strategy

Corporate Strategy

The first Strategic Planning consideration for management, involves the combined efforts of different management functions.

First: Marketing will have researched the intended markets, identifying the wants and needs of the potential customers.

Next: together with the Technical function, Marketing will decide those company products that will satisfy the market.

Then: with the Finance and other Logistics functions, including Purchasing, they will verify that the products can be made, stored and distributed at a *profit*.

This is fundamental for company strategic planning, as is recognition of the organization's "core competences", or *what it does best*. What a company *does best*, may be a successful business activity of theirs, for which the company was not set up in the first place!

A good example of this is the Maguire and Paterson company, set up in 1882 to make matches. This they did, for generations, producing matches of a quality better, or on a par with the world's best. Ninety years later, the demand for matches changed. People were smoking less. Cheap disposable lighters were being imported. Having carried out a *SWOT* analysis on themselves and their market, they identified their core competences - *what they did best.* And, what they *did best* was *Distribution. Where can you **not** buy a box of their matches conveniently?* Starting with Wilkinson Sword Razors they acquired many agencies for prestigious products that could be distributed through the same channels as matches. Today they are a top Distribution company.

A *SWOT* analysis exercise carried out by an organization, identifies the company's Strengths, Weaknesses, Opportunities and Threats.
By applying this *SWOT* analysis approach to customers, suppliers, competitors, and the company itself, an organization puts itself in the position of making better decisions, from the better information so acquired.

Three Objectives of Corporate Strategy

To identify and analyse the organization's core competences, the requirements of customers, the strengths of competitors, the firm's financial restraints and thereby to be in the best position to maximise profits by setting and achieving objectives to:

1. Prepare a sound base from which to develop the company and staff over the long term,
2. To be ahead of the competition in knowing what the markets actually need,
3. To design, or redesign, products to satisfy those needs together with the essential proactive support of the Logistics function.

Logistics Strategy and Planning are part of the overall strategic direction for the company.
Logistics Planning decisions involve

(a) the location of warehouses or wholesalers,
(b) setting inventory control policies and procedures,
(c) developing customer service units,
(d) designing order entry systems,
(e) evaluating distribution networks,
(f) setting customer service levels, and
(g) choosing modes of transport.

Logistics Strategy revolves around the three essential objectives of Cost reduction, Capital reduction, and Service development

1. *Cost reduction*. There are certain *fixed* costs in Logistics activities such as the leasing charges for vehicles, and the stores heating and lighting expenses. *Variable* costs are often in danger of getting out of control. However, variable costs including fuel, tyres, overtime working, pallet replacement, and scrap, if controlled systematically can be reduced effectively.

2. *Capital reduction*. Stock costs money to hold and if: (a) stock levels *throughout the distribution network*, are monitored and kept to optimum figures, and (b) JIT ("just in time") delivery systems are installed for high usage value items, *the cost of storage can be reduced considerably.*
Shipping finished goods directly from Production to customers eliminates stock holding costs. This is an object of JIT manufacturing.

3. *Service development*. To a large extent competition determines the price a firm charges in the market place and also the *level of service supplied.* Service improvement can be effected by increasing the stock held in store, but at a cost. It is important to check and see if the extra profit expected from increased sales, due to holding a higher service level, compensates for the extra cost of storage.

Logistics Planning Basics involve three time-horizons.

Strategic Planning or long term
Tactical Planning usually covering one year, and
Operational Planning or the day to day decisions that have to be taken..

There are four major areas covered in Logistics Planning.

1. Facility location.
2. Inventory decisions.
3. Customer Service Level - CSL.
4. Transport decisions.

Major Areas	Strategic	Tactical	Operational
Facility Location	*Number of Regional Wholesalers*	*N/A*	*N/A*
Inventory Decisions	*Distribution Channel and controls*	*Buffer-Stock Levels*	*Customer Order Filling*
CSL-Customer Service Level	*Policy Statement*	*Agree max-min Levels*	*Set up trial Levels*
Transport Decisions	*Mode Selection*	*Seasonal Vehicle Hire*	*Delivering*

Four major areas covered in Logistics Planning

4 Packaging

The Purpose

The Storage, Transportation and Distribution of materials, require them to be handled and moved securely and safely, without damage to themselves, or to surrounding materials; *and* without injury to personnel involved at any stage of this process. *This is the overall purpose of Packaging.*

There are very few products, such as motor-cars, items of furniture, or bulk raw materials, which are *not* distributed in packages.

Definition:

"Packaging is the general term used to cover all aspects of the *protective* use of materials and related procedures, in the adequate preparation of goods for safe handling, storage, marketing and despatch, *up to a suitable standard* enabling the purchaser to have full enjoyment of the contents as a legal Right".

Of necessity, this standard must ensure the following:

(a) inclusion of correct and adequate labelling of containers and wrappers; and

(b) exclusion of the use of : *fire inducing*, *fire sustaining*, and TARHaG (*thermally activated release of hazardous gas*) materials; in the manufacture of packages and packing, padding and filling materials - as used in furniture.

Packaging and our Standard of Living; one everyday example:

Many foodstuffs are now available year-round due to new packaging and conservation techniques. *Packaging* has been devised which offers protection against oxygen, light, condensation, other food odours and flavours. The taste of the product can be guaranteed consistent up to the final use-by date. Packaging has become synonymous with our modern way of living.

Responsibility - the move from Production to Marketing

Packaging, which at one time was thought of as being a *Production* function, is now rightfully regarded as the vehicle from which a product is to be sold; and as such, must provide attractiveness and protection for the contents.

More and more manufacturers and distributors have come to realize that safe delivery of a well-protected quality product, which can meet heavy sales competition, demands Packaging that is economical, attractive, and is well fitted for its purpose.

Packaging the Product

The use of *packaging* as part of marketing policy, depends on the type of product and its targeted end user:

(a) "Industrial Goods or Materials" is the description for, raw materials, maintenance items, consumables, and capital items (e.g. plant & machinery), sold directly to manufacturers. However, with capital equipment; packaging priorities are maximum protection and safety in movement, rather than the appearance of the package.

(b) "Consumer Goods" is the usual description given to finished products sold to the general public, like food and washing powder which have a "short life". "Consumer Durables" is the description for "longer life" items such as furniture, TVs, cars, and certain clothes. In the consumer field, the visual impact of the package for the "short-life product" is a packaging priority where an increasing number of products are competing for the consumer's eye, and especially for his or her money. A package is useful for putting over the company *logo*. A logo gives a product an identity that is readily recognized by the consumer.

Packaging and New Product Design

Consideration should be given to *packaging*, during the development stage of a product. All too often, the packaging is considered after the product has been developed.
The package should be part of the *product concept*.
Quite often, there are *conflicting needs* of packer, distributor, and consumer or industrial end user, which have to be met. If discussed at the design stage, these needs will not become major problems difficult to solve later.

Packaging the Product and Purchasing

Purchasing should be involved in discussions on, and decisions about, packaging, from day one.
Chemical composition of the proposed package, EU legislation, the Green impact, are but some of the considerations which are better handled in the early stages of package design, rather than as part of a "correction" exercise when purchase orders need to be placed.
Early involvement by Purchasing will enable cost reducing techniques of Value Engineering, and on-going Value Analysis to be implemented.

Legal Aspects of Packaging:

Pre 1980

"Provided the goods are of 'Merchantable Quality' and 'Fit for the purpose', we have discharged our duty regardless of the condition or suitability of the containers in which they are packaged."
This was the stance of many suppliers into the 1970s.

After 1980

This argument has been discredited by Case Law since the mid 1980s, whether the containers are sold with the goods, hired,suplied on loan, or are returnable.
In principle, the containers, of whatever kind, from boxes to bottles, and cartons to cases, must be such as *to enable the purchaser to have full enjoyment of the contents.*
If the reader will excuse the pun, ***Packaging is part and parcel of the product.***

Using Suppliers' Packaging - Safety Aspects
If the Industrial Purchaser wishes to store the goods in the original container(s), or on the pallets supplied, he or she would be wise to inform the supplier of this, *and obtain advice.*
For example, some goods, delivered on pallets could be safely stacked five pallets high, while other goods must be stacked no more than three pallets high.

Incorrect Labelling
Inadequate or incorrect product labelling, by a supplier or manufacturer, as well as being in breach of Section 14 of the Sale of Goods Act, may result in an end user's successful claim for negligence.
The omission of details of hazards related to the transport, use and storage of chemicals could contravene the Hazardous Substances or other legislation. Before finalizing packaging choice at new product design stage, companies should consult *impending* as well as current packaging legislation.

Environment and Packaging Waste
Since December 1994, when the EU passed into law their "Packaging and Packaging Waste Directive" mandatory recycling schemes have been set up in member states. The Irish "Waste Management (Packaging) Regulations came into effect on July 1st 1997. (S.I. No. 242 of 1997 refers)

5 Packaging and the Environment

Ideally, *packaging* should be "Environment-Friendly", bio-degradable or recyclable.

Peoples' Attitudes.

Surveys in the US and in the EU, have repeatedly shown that many consumers claim to conscientiously buy products packaged in "Environment-Friendly "material. In reality, however, the market shows that the consumer does not buy "green", to the extent imagined; although he or she has the *will* to do so.

As a direct result of the Greens opening discussions in 1990 on "packaging as a waste problem", there was almost immediate activity by politicians, many of them appearing to be genuinely concerned. Very soon, legal steps were taken with the purpose of reducing the amount of packaging waste.

- Germany introduced the Packaging Ordinance in 1991.
- The Netherlands soon followed, with the Packaging Covenant.
- France introduced their Eco Emballage.
- Belgium introduced the Eco Tax.
- The EU, in December 1994, passed into law their "Packaging and Packaging Waste Directive." (96/62/EC of 20th December 1994, refers)
- Governments world-wide, are implementing legislation to protect the environment from packaging and packaging waste.

Dáil Éireann passed its Bill on Packaging Waste through both houses of the Oireachtas in 1996, *as per the 1994 EU Directive on packaging and packaging waste - (1).*
Framework legislation was enacted in May 1996, and the main provisions were brought into force on 1st July 1996. The Minister for the Environment, in exercise of powers conferred on him by this 1996 Waste Management Act, made a series of regulations that were operative from July 1st 1997. These are called Waste Management (Packaging) Regulations, 1997, and Waste Management (Farm Plastics) Regulations, 1997.

* **As reported in "European Purchasing and Materials Management" page 262, Issue No. 7. 1996.**

Packaging Waste Management - 1997 Regulations

Introduction

The 1994 EU Directive is causing mandatory recycling schemes to appear in member states. In the UK, industries prompted by the government, have accepted responsibility for designing RFSs - recycling funding schemes. In Germany, companies have to pay a levy of DM3 per kg., on every *plastic* package that they sell. *Ironically, this may be more than the cost of the raw material used to manufacture the container!*

This directive has set the focus for Marketing, Technical, and Purchasing, not only on *recyclability*, but also on package or packing re-design; often to the point of product modification or change:

(a) in Germany Beecham removed cartons from toothpaste tubes, and sales increased.

(b) Proctor and Gamble have successfully produced concentrated washing detergents to reduce product packaging.

It appears that if the *Functionality* of the packaging, *which is concerned with protection of the product, end user safety, convenience, and package attractiveness,* is not compromised, then the end user will accept changes to protect the environment.

The Waste Management (Packaging) Regulations, 1997 are designed to promote the ***Recovery*** of packaging waste. These Regulations place new obligations on persons and businesses who supply packaging (i.e. packaging materials, packaging or packaged goods) to the Irish market. These businesses can be manufacturers, converters, packer/fillers, distributors, wholesalers or retailers. These obligations are designed to assist and promote the recycling of packaging waste, so that Ireland will meet the packaging waste recovery targets laid down in the EU Directive 94/62/EC on packaging and packaging waste. A successful performance for Ireland depends on the sum-total of Irish company performances in recycling, reclaiming and re-using packaging waste.

"Recovery", *in relation to waste, is the term used to describe any activity carried out to reclaim, recycle or otherwise reuse the waste in whole or in part.*

Do the Regulations Apply to All Companies?
The regulations apply to *all "producers"* but especially to *"major producers"* of packaging.

What is meant by the terms "producer" and "major producer" of packaging?
A *"producer"* of packaging is a company or person who, in the course of trade or business, imports, manufactures, sells or otherwise supplies to other companies or persons, packaging, packaging material or packaged goods. This covers companies which

1. supply the raw materials for the manufacture of packaging.
2. manufacture various packaging materials, or
3. convert or otherwise process materials into packaging,
4. fill or put products into packaging, or
5. sell packaged products, whether as distributors or retailers.

A *"major producer"* is a producer of packaging whose annual SVT (sales value turnover), *including export sales*, is in excess of IR£1million, *AND* who annually places an excess of 25 tonnes of packaging on the Irish market, *excluding packaging destined for reuse*.**
The tonnage figure is a total of packaging output from all premises of the producer.
(The weight of exported packaging is, of course, excluded from the calculations.)

Requirements of the Regulations - What must a "Producer" do?
Assist the recovery of packaging waste arising on the company's own premises.
All producers have these obligations to carry out:

- *return* the packaging to a supplier, or
- *recover* it, or arrange for its *recovery*, or
- *segregate* it, offer it free of charge to recyclers and store it for at least four weeks pending collection by a recycler.

Major producers have to effect additional obligations.

- Submit a plan to the relevant local authority(ies) detailing the company's procedures for complying with the regulations.
- Register with the said local authority(ies), every premises of the company, from which packaging is issued. (Application fees are a minimum of IR£200 to a maximum of IR£1000 per premises).
- Display a notice on each premises indicating that packaging waste *of the type placed on the market by the producer*, will be accepted, free of charge (Article 5).
  [Suppose there are two breakfast cereal manufacturers - A and B. The cartons (classified as paper) and boxes, (now waste), from A's sales to the market, or any paper (e.g. newspapers) from any source will be accepted by B].
- Accept from any person any waste packaging *of the type supplied by the producer* (Article 5).
- Collect (upon request) packaging waste from any other producer to whom packaging or packaged products were supplied, (i.e. from *customers* of the producer who are also producers).

** **"Packaging destined for reuse" means packaging which has been conceived and designed to accomplish within its life cycle a minimum of two *closed trip rotations between customer and supplier.*"**

Requirements of the Regulations (continued)

Having accepted or collected the packaging, the producer now has to:

1 Arrange for a *supplier of such material* to take away the packaging, OR
Recover the packaging or arrange for a *bona fide* recovery operator to do so, OR
Segregate and store the waste for a minimum of four weeks, thereby facilitating offering the packaging to *recovery operators* free of charge. If this offer for recycling is not taken up within the four weeks, the waste can be disposed of in a suitable manner.

2 Maintain records of packaging produced, packaging waste recovered, and contacts with recovery operators, as per Article 7. Provide a monthly report for the relevant local authority.

5.Provide an annual report of *performance* to the relevant local authority *and make it available to the public.*

What Companies Must Do and How They Can Measure Performance

Companies are required to accept packaging, *of the type which they use*, up to 100% of the amount which they themselves placed on the market in any one month.
One measurement system that can be used then, is to express the weight of packaging waste accepted by the company as a percentage of the total weight of packaging put into the system by that company in the same month or period.

Companies are required to collect, or arrange to have collected up to 100% of the packaging or packaging material, *of the type supplied by them* to another producer, within one week of being requested to do so. This creates another Performance measurement system - *expressing the quantity of packaging waste collected by the company from another producer or other producers, as a percentage of the total quantity supplied by them to the same or different producers, in the same month or period.*

Those companies which Pack or Fill products into packaging, or import packaged goods for resale, are required to accept packaging up to a minimum of 40% of the amount which they place on the market in any one month. If this quantity of packaging waste is not returned to them by their customers or others, *they are required to make-up the shortfall* by contracting with another party, or arranging a collection system for waste packaging. Again this gives rise to a Performance measurement system

Retailers *must provide convenient facilities for their customers to deposit or return packaging.*

Is There An Alternative and Easier Way To Comply With The Regulations? Yes!

The regulations require suppliers of packaging, to implement procedures themselves to assist the *"recovery"* of packaging waste as outlined, or *to participate in a packaging waste recovery scheme operated by an approved body.*

Who are the Approved Bodies?

Initially, and for the foreseeable future, there is only one approved body for the purpose of the Regulations - *Repak Ltd., Kylemore Road, Dublin,10. Tel (01) 623 7747 Fax (01) 623 7748*
Repak Ltd., is a non profit-making private limited company set up under a voluntary agreement between Industry and the Department of the Environment, with in-put from Local Government. It is committed to achieving a collection and recycling level of 27% of packaging waste on behalf of its members. It operates with a CEO and a small staff, sub-contracting out its recycling activities.
The Repak packaging waste recovery scheme is open to membership by all suppliers of packaging. ***Membership of the Repak scheme will exempt companies from many obligations under the 1997 legislation.***

Major *"producers"* of packaging are required to display a notice indicating, as appropiate, that they are either:

(a) ***required** to accept packaging waste, or*
(b) *are a member of Repak and are **not required** to accept packaging waste.*

Repak Services
Repak provides its members with important services.

- Members of Repak are exempt from the obligations imposed on companies under the Packaging Waste Legislations, but are obliged to comply with Repak membership rules.

- Repak members do not have to take back waste from their customers nor do they have to contribute towards any other collection or recycling scheme

- Repak assumes responsibility for the recovery of packaging waste from the domestic sector on industry's behalf. It does this in a cost effective manner by using the funds it collects to subsidize collection schemes from households.

- Repak liaises with Government Local Authorities, Environmental Protection Agencies and other relevant bodies, on behalf of its members.

  Repak will provide telephone guidance and advice to its members on all aspects of packaging waste.

- Repak issues the necessary membership certificates for Regulations exemptions.

Currently, membership fees are related to SVT (sales value turnover), e.g. an annual fee of IR£2000 for companies with an SVT between IR£5m to IR£10m.
Eventually fees will be based on the *amount* and *types* of packaging waste put into the Market.

Obligations on Repak Members

Members of Repak are obluged to:

- Fund Repak Activities.
- Provide data in confidence on the weight of packaging put into the market and the packaging waste arising internally.
- Deal responsibility with waste packaging arising on their premises, i.e.
  separate waste into individual material groups,
  contract with waste contractor to have packaging placed into a recycling stream.
  obtain and keep for a 5 year period, copies of weight-bridge tickets and recycling certificates.

In addition, members of Repak will have to internalize the costs associated in dealing with their in-house waste packaging

Repak Membership Costs

Turnover IR£ millions	Category A - F	Annual Fee IR£
1 - 5	A	1,000 + Vat
5 - 10	B	2,000 +Vat
10 - 20	C	5,000 + Vat
20 - 50	D	10,000 + Vat
50 - 100	E	15,000 + Vat
Over 100	F	20,000 + Vat

Ireland's National Recovery Targets are defined as follows:

(1). A minimum of 27% by weight of all packaging waste to be recycled by June 2001.
(2). 50% - 65% by weight of packaging waste to be recycled before the end of 2005.
and
(3). A minimum recycling rate of 15% by weight of each material grouping.

6 Packaging, Product Characteristics and Transport

The Functions of Packaging:

The raison d'être or purpose of packaging can be divided into two functional categories: primary and secondary. The primary functions are obvious to the majority of us; most of the secondary functions escape us at first thought, but they also become obvious, once our attention is drawn to them.

Primary Functions of Packaging:

(1) To *protect* the goods from the environment in which they are moved and stored; *and of course when relevant, to protect the environment from the material being moved or stored.*

(2) To enable the product to be handled, stored, marketed, despatched and transported, safely, conveniently, without loss or damage to the contents; as economically as possible.

Secondary Functions of Packaging:

(1) To provide a convenient method of selling goods in acceptable weights and quantities.
(2) To identify the goods.
(3) To provide a convenient method of dispensing products in prescribed doses; e.g. medication in time - release capsules.

(4) To permit the safe handling, storage, and transportation of hazardous commodities;
(5) To carry safety instructions for the handling and use of hazardous or potentially harmful products; and display first-aid advice in the event of an accident
(6) To protect the environment during transportation of hazardous substances.

(7) To carry technical instructions for the correct use of the product.
(8) To carry advertizing matter, logos, brand images, or trade names.
(9) To give the product sales appeal and shelf appeal

(10) To provide a hygienic method of handling, storing, transporting, food and medicines
(11) To preserve the life of the product
(12) To prevent or greatly reduce the likelihood of pilferage.

(13) To guard against product deterioration due to climatic conditions, insect or rodent attack.
(14) To protect the contents from tampering by the use of, e.g. child-proof closures.

Materials used in Packaging:

Common materials from which packaging is made are; paper board, metals, wood, plywood, plastic of many varieties including: polystyrene, polyethylene, PVC, nylon, and the still popular glass. Bonded laminates and composite materials are also used. *Technically, paint, grease, and other barrier films can also be regarded as packaging materials; as in the protection of metals from rusting.*

Product Characteristics - Impact on Packaging and Transportation

The characteristics of the product influence the development and operation of the Logistics system.

A list of typical characteristics includes: weight, volume, value, perishability, fragility, hazard, and substitutability.

These attributes can be classified and discussed under four headings:

1. *Packaging and product density, i.e.volume-weight ratio,or weight-bulk ratio),*
2. *Value-weight ratio,*
3. *Substitutability, and*
4. *Special risk characteristics.*

1. Packaging and Product Density - Volume to Weight Ratio

One is reminded of the school teacher's trick question: "which is heavier, a tonne of feathers or a tonne of bricks?" While the weight is the same, the volume of the feathers is considerable in comparison to the volume of the bricks.

Here, we are looking at the *weight-bulk ratio*, or as it is usually called, *the volume to weight ratio*.

This ratio is a very important measure of what influences the costs of storage, transportation and distribution. Products that have a high density, i.e. *a low volume to weight ratio* (such as sheet steel, books, canned paint) permit efficient use of storage, transportation and distribution.

The converse of this; products that have a low density, i.e. a *high volume to weight ratio* (such as crisps, paper tissues, cut flowers and, *those feathers*), incur high costs for storage, transportation and distribution. Handling costs are greater for low density items than for high density ones.

Being aware of this factor in computing storage and transportation costs, some firms have made fundamental changes in their product design. Some fabricators push final assembly as far up the distribution chain as possible. Examples of this are desk manufacturers and steel storage-rack manufacturers, who ship their product in high density "knocked-down" form for assembly by distributors.

In the UK (and formerly in Ireland), MFI Ltd have extensive showrooms of furniture on display.

A housewife impressed by a beautiful sofa on display, orders one and is presented with a rectangular box of parts complete with instructions for later assembly in her home, (by an "enthusiastic" husband). *The potential savings on transportation costs of shipping high density products, requires marketing and logistics people to co-operate in package redesign.*

Product Characteristics (continued)
2. Transport and the Value-Weight Ratio

Transportation costs are related to the weight of the product being shipped, not the value. *It may be possible to change packaging requirements to reduce the gross weight of products.* When the value of the consignment is low, the transportation charge is a high percentage of the actual delivered home cost. It is often prudent then to carry high stocks of low value items, (their "cost of storage" also being low), so that fewer purchase orders are placed for transportation. This would entail being prepared to accept longer lead-times by using seafreight, rather than using faster but expensive airfreight. Again a "just-in-time" - JIT system for deliveries of *high value-weight* materials is recommended. The extra transport costs involved in more frequent deliveries of smaller purchase-order sizes, could not justify this JIT method for *low value-weight* materials.

3. Transport and Substitutability

Products are said to have low-substitutability or high-substitutability.

High-substitutability:

A mother sending her child on an errand says; ". . . and if they haven't got Barry's get Lyons",
[or if you prefer; ". . . and if they haven't got Lyons get Barry's"]

High-substitutability describes a branded product which is not regarded by the average customer as being *the one and only product worth buying* in any supply situation. *It is the case where a customer is willing to buy a second choice brand, when the first is not readily available.* A good example of a product like this is *white paint.* Manufacturers and Distributors, considering the *value-weight ratio,* could *increase the frequency of product deliveries* to avoid stock-outs throughout the distribution chain, thereby removing the need for the customer to consider a substitute. To prevent or reduce lost sales, the firm's *transportation policy* could be revised to allow for occasional *"less than economic load sizes";* resulting from the increased frequency of product deliveries. An Integrated Logistics system would make this easier to achieve, by the cooperation of all managers concerned.

Low-substitutability:

Service Manager says to the courier company; "and we must have that car part here by 2.00 pm today".

Low-substitutability describes a branded product that is usually the one and only choice of a customer. Only occasionally will a substitute product be acceptable. An example of this would be the top selling soft drinks, where customers reluctantly buy another brand if their first choice is out of stock.

Product Characteristics (continued)
4. Special Risk Characteristics
There are six basic potential risks associated with the transport and distribution of a product. Sometimes expensive specialized transport or distribution systems need to be involved.

Risk Factors Include:	***Necessary Requirements Include:***
(a) Perishability,	Refrigerated storage and vehicle required.
(b) Fragility	Special packaging to protect against shocks.
(c) Flammability, or other hazard,	Special regulations, limited load size, special labelling, Isolation from other products.
(d) Ease of contamination,	Specially sealed outer packaging.
(e) High value,	Secure means of distribution.
(f) Ease of theft.	Special care in handling, use specialist couriers.

7 The Package and The Product

The Package - first principles
As has been emphasised earlier, the package should be considered as *part of the idea* of a new product. Before a package can be chosen or designed, the *product characteristics* as listed above need to be identified and *three assessments* carried out.

Product Assessments
Assessment (1) The Product (i.e. the proposed contents of the package)

Method: Identify the product properties chosen from this or a similar list.

Physical: Form; dimensions; size, weight, density, specific gravity, rigidity, fragility, stability, unit quantity(ies) to be packed, stored, transported, surface finish (e.g. rough or sharp) and cost.

Chemical: Susceptibility to water, moisture vapour, heat or cold, oxygen, flavours odours; or/and other factors specific to the proposed contents in question.
Certain chemical products may require a packaging specification laid down by statutory regulations.
Airlines often require chemical products to be packed in small containers (1 litre), which must then be individually surrounded by inert absorbent material, within an outer carton.

Product Assessments (continued)
Assessment (2) The Proposed Marketing Technique.

Information is required as to how the product is to be distributed.

Direct to end user; or through one or more distribution channels.
The greater the number of channels, the greater the number of times the packaged product will be handled. This will determine the strength quality needed for the package.

Assessment (3) The Proposed Handling, Storage, and Transportation Conditions.

Handling: The type of equipment used, FLTs, cranes, conveyors, all dictate the required strength needed in a product's package.

Storage: The methods of loading and unloading a product, and the number of likely movements to and from storage areas, will be another indication of the strength of the packaging required

Transport. The mode of transport to be used, e.g. road or rail.
Goods moved by road are loaded and unloaded only once, whereas goods sent by rail could be moved up to twelve times, dramatically increasing the risk of damage to the product if not packaged adequately.

Goods may be exposed to rough treatment if shipped as part of a mixed consignment.
When part of a full container load there is less likelihood of damage.
Light outer packaging is adequate for goods shipped by air transport.

Other Points:
It may be necessary to ascertain, accurately, the conditions of humidity, temperature, and time to which goods are likely to be exposed.
Size and shape, also need to be considered in the context of unit load density; e.g. square containers take up less space than cylindrical ones.

The Requirements of a Package:

We have seen that the design of a package depends on many factors. The following list includes the basic requirements, essential and common to most packages.

(1) Safety of personnel. Not just the safety of the product end-user; but ALL personnel involved with the package, from manufacturing to finished product filling (or wrapping), to distribution to storing, to despatch, to recycling or destruction.
(2) Easy to fill.
(3) Easy to empty.

(4) Secure closure: convenient but safe to open and close.
(5) The material from which the package is made, must be *compatible* with the proposed contents. It should not be harmful to the environment during the package - manufacturing process, or in the package - destruction process at its end life.
(6) Clear identification of contents, and clear display of weight or volume.

(7) To comply with labelling and other legal regulations on potentially dangerous materials *including additives in food.*
(8) Adequate strength for handling, storage, and transportation, as per the needs of Marketing.
(9) Capable of being handled by the envisaged methods, manual and mechanical. Loads despatched, must be suitably packed for customers' unloading facilities.

(10) Adequate resistance from exposure to contaminants.
(11) To show a Sell-by (Use-by) date.
(12) To display a batch number.

(13) Attractive appearance.
(14) Cushioning of fragile items.
(15) Separation of inner contents if liable to damage by friction or vibration in transit.

(16) Support for the product; e.g. an egg tray.
(17) To withstand pressure changes in aircraft.
(18) To act as a barrier to light and solar radiation.

(19) To act as a barrier to radio-activity in laboratories, hospitals, or in industry.
(20) "Reuse packaging" (e.g. returnable cartons), need to be made of a robust material.

8 Materials Handling - Its Aims, Functions and Importance

Materials Handling - a Definition

"Techniques employed to move, transport, store or distribute materials (whether liquid or solid) with or without the aid of mechanical appliances". (BSI definition.)

Storage and handling systems are evolving and developing in two ways:

(a) through technically advanced mechanisation and automation systems (e.g. Robotics), which reduce manpower, eliminate fatigue, increase the speed of response, and improve reliability.

(b) through advances made in IT - information technology.

Aim and Functions of Materials Handling

The aim of Materials Handling is to ensure safe convenient and orderly flow throughout the stores.

(1) Movement of materials to and from storage and inter-department transporting.

(2) Selection of materials, checking measurement, weight or volume.

(3) Customer (internal or external) order filling, assembling material quantities.

(4) Loading and unloading.

Importance of a Materials Handling System

Materials Handling is regarded as a major and costly activity in stores, warehouses, stock-yards and in manufacturing or processing plants. Manual handling and mechanical handling are two methods of moving, carrying, and storing materials. Manual handling is always an option to be considered in the choice of some handling systems. Many old warehouses were constructed before the conception of modern mechanical handling equipment. Manual handling equipment, like the pallet truck, is efficient and easy to use. Having a manual barrel-lift, is a great advantage to firms handling liquid raw materials. Items of mechanical handling equipment, despite the often large financial outlay, and the essential need for staff training in their safe use; are common-place in most stores and manufacturing plants, so much so, that the plants could not exist without them.

The importance paid to Materials Handling in an organization is indicated by the degree of financial commitment given to the equipment.

The Choice of Suitable Materials Handling Equipment

Choice as part of the overall system, should result in:

(1) reduction of costly double-handling,

(2) saving time; issues to production are more easily effected, as is

(3) the quicker preparation of order-despatch to customers,

(4) although requiring wider aisles than manual handling systems, a mechanized high-stacking equipment system will save storage space,

(5) some labour can be deployed to other stores duties,

An efficient Materials Handling system will result in moving the right goods, safely, to the right place, at the right time, and at the right cost.

Materials Handling - System Selection

Just as with modern concepts of Marketing, where potential customers' wants and needs must first be identified prior to thoughts of new product design; the successful selection of a materials handling system must first consider a number of key factors - *internal and external* - and seek answers to the following questions:

External factors: Will suppliers' materials handling systems have any bearing on the firm's choice of equipment?
Will customers' materials handling systems affect the choice likewise?

Internal factors: Does the warehouse design impose choice restrictions - narrow aisles multi-storey building, separate buildings far apart?
Are throughput volumes and handling characteristics of the product mix constant?
Substantial heavy volume indicates a choice for mechanical equipment, the converse indicating manual equipment.
Will choice need to consider requirements of Production?
What are the nature and characteristics of the materials to be handled?
Will system selected be flexible enough to accommodate future needs?
Using a terotechnologial approach, what is the total cost of each proposed system?
What are acquisition options available? Use capital resources to buy or lease.

Information Technology and Materials Handling Systems

The number of computer applications to assist the overall Logistics function continues to increase. As a minimum, computers are used to record information on;

(a) *material receipts*,
(b) *quality inspection*,
(c) *storage*,
(d) *production issues*; and
(e) *customer despatches of materials.*

These materials movements are linked to bar coding of pallets - or even individual cartons and boxes - ensuring that operators of Materials Handling equipment work efficiently and economically.
FLTs can have on-board-computers to facilitate real time data input and information receipt.

Effects of a badly managed Materials-Handling system:

An efficient Materials Handling system is an essential part of all manufacturing and warehousing operations. If the system is badly managed, untold harm can accrue to the organization, with results like the following:

(1) Excessive delays.

(a) Excessive unloading delays in the receiving of raw materials.

As well as affecting the organization, suppliers will soon complain about their delivery schedules being disrupted. After a few delays, supplier's drivers (or their haulier's drivers), will place the organization in last place on their delivery roster.

This of course, will cause many problems for the organization's buyer. It could be the cause of problems in future supplier-negotiations. .

(b) Excessive delays to the flow of materials on the manufacturing line.

This will result in bottlenecks and creation of large WIP - work in progress - stocks.

(c) Excessive delays in selecting and marshalling goods for despatch and distribution.

Delays of this sort, in many peoples' minds, are "just short of being criminal", because they affect the organization's customers. All the costly efforts of Sales and Marketing to persuade customers to buy the organization's product, could easily be put to nought.

(2) Goods being damaged within the stores and production line.

(3) Poor utilization of space in the warehouse.

(4) Laxity in the areas of administration, training, (especially of young or new employees), and of supervision. As well as contributing to, or creating the problems detailed above, this laxity inevitability leads to different forms of bad housekeeping, and neglect of safety procedures

33% of accidents in the work-place result from manual handling, (IBEC video).

A few successful claims for negligence, taken against an organization, could put that firm out of business with the loss of all jobs; maybe yours!

Safety is everybody's responsibility!

Causes of Inefficiency in Materials Handling

Following from what we have read in the last seven sections, we can now list out the major causes of an inefficient Materials-Handling system.

- Absence of adequate financial commitment given by the organization to equipment purchase
- Goods frequently moved to wrong locations
- Ad hoc purchasing of equipment - no such thing as strategic planning
- Manual equipment having to cater for high volumes
- No consideration given to advantages of computer - bar coding of pallets
- Slow unloading of deliveries, slow storage, leading to delays of materials flow to production
- An absence of good housekeeping

9 Materials Handling - Introduction to Equipment

Materials Handling/Storage, and Loading Bay Equipment

Manual/ Mechanical Handling - Introduction:

Many of the world's enduring structures were constructed with the muscle power of hundreds of men and women. The earliest form of materials-handling equipment was probably the tree trunk; used as both a roller and a lever. Later, the combination of the newly invented wheel and animal power - oxen, mules, elephants, or horses - dominated materials handling until the advent of steam power.

The discovery of new uses for electricity and the invention of the combustion engine, widened the whole conceptual scope of materials handling. Today, the range of mechanical handling equipment on the market is almost endless. There is usually a good choice of standard equipment available to a firm; or that firm can have equipment built to its specification, to suit a special need.

However, the option of manual handling should always be considered for any handling system.

Movement Equipment Choice - Manual and Mechanical

Some firms regard it essential to have materials handling equipment permanently on site. Others may only need to hire a pallet truck or an FLT on an occasional basis.

The Main Types of Manual Handling Equipment are:

1. Four-wheeled platform trucks
2. Two-wheeled hand trucks
3. Hand pallet trucks
4. Selection trolleys, including "intelligent" trolleys with self scanning
5. Sack wheel-barrows

Low cost and flexibility make manual equipment ideally suitable for *low-throughput-volume* stores.

The Main Types of Mechanical Handling Equipment are:

1. Lift trucks
2. Tractors
3. Hand trucks and carts
4. Powered Pallet Trucks
5. Powered Stackers
6. Order Picking trucks for either Low, Medium or High levels
7. Conveyors and Cranes
8. Miscellaneous items such as chutes, pulley blocks, lifts and scissors lifts
9. Under-floor conveyors. Loads are carried on trolleys that engage with a continuous motor driven chain running inside floor channels. There is no interference with traffic over the floor.
10. AGVs (automatic guided vehicles) are driverless trolleys guided over a predetermined route by
    (a) following signals transmitted through an underfloor "loop" or wire, or
    (b) by optically reading a painted line or plastic tape track on the floor, or
    (c) by a radio controlled version of the above, allowing for multi-direction travel within a dedicated area or
11. Robots - *the use of computer controlled robots* that can undertake consistent, fast, "handling" operations, with a high degree of both safety and quality performance, is likely to increase

10 Types of Fork Lift Trucks (FLTs)

Power-Assisted Equipment

The development of the FLT, has had as great an affect on materials handling, as did the invention of the wheel. The lift truck has been called the workhorse of the stores. Most stores have at least one lift truck. It is probably the most versatile single piece of equipment used in the stores, and many use them exclusively. It can move things horizontally and vertically; and it can travel about freely. With special attachments it can pick up, turn, push and pull all types and shapes of objects.

Because of the importance the lift truck plays in materials handling, considerable effort and money have been invested in developing its basic design, to make it as flexible in use as possible. There is a broad selection of FLT designs to choose from. The many attachments available, extend the utility and versatility of the basic machines.

Basic Fork Lift Truck Designs:

(a) Counterbalance Type:

The maid-of-all-work among fork lift trucks, highly stable, fitted with *large tyre wheels,* can work outdoors and on moderate gradients. It uses the principle of counterbalance whereby the load being carried is balanced by the weight of the machine with the front wheels acting as a fulcrum. The design permits trucks to be made with almost an unlimited lift capacity and reach height.

(b) Reach Trucks:

With this design of truck the load is carried within the wheel base. The lift mechanism usually incorporates a reach mechanism to enable the load to be stored or picked up outside the wheel base. Reach trucks can operate in aisles as little as two thirds of the width of those required by counterbalanced trucks. Their smaller wheels and different design make them less suitable for general purpose rough work.

(c) Narrow Aisle Trucks:

These in turn require less aisle space than the reach trucks. They handle pallets in narrow aisle racking without turning in the aisle. They use telescopic forks, rotating forks, and rotating masts. These trucks are frequently guided by special rails. Handling within the aisles can be very rapid. It is generally wasteful to use these expensive trucks outside the racking, although some models with lower lift heights can be used occasionally for more general work. New style compact 24 volt battery electric, three-wheeler FLTs, with a clear view mast are available for narrow aisle work.

(d) VNA Trucks:

These are a further development of the original Narrow Aisle Truck, which permit the use of new VNA storage racking systems. These specialized FLTs are used to move boxed or paletted goods between racks which can be both narrow and very high.

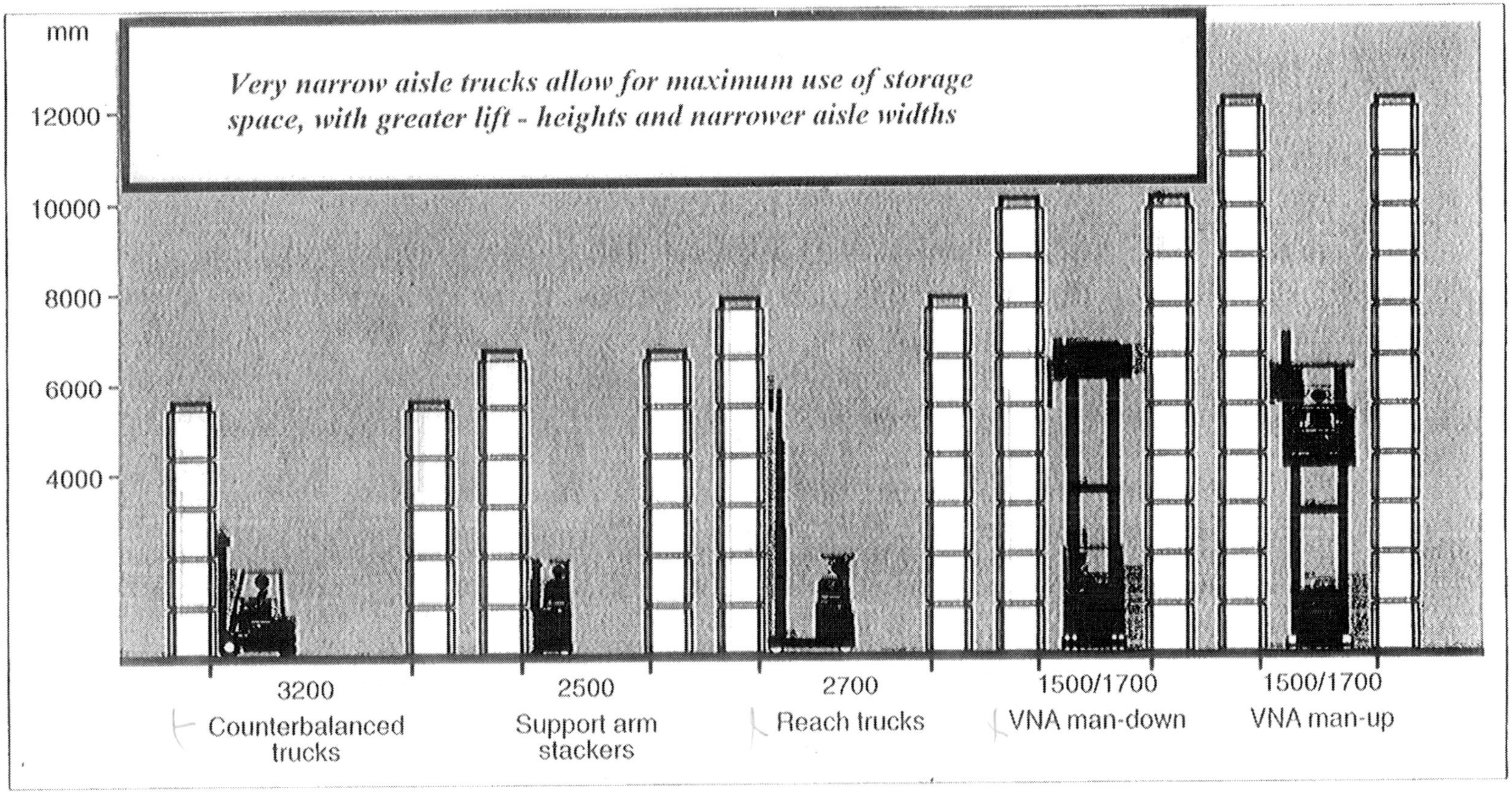

Chart and illustrations courtesy of **BT Rolatruc**

Seán de Foirc says

"Bí cúramach i gcónaí - use the correct way to lift a pallet out of a rack"

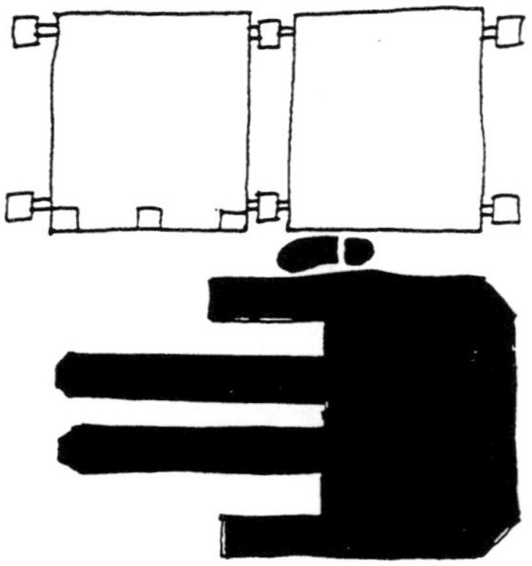

The support arm wheel a foot's width from the corner of the pallet.

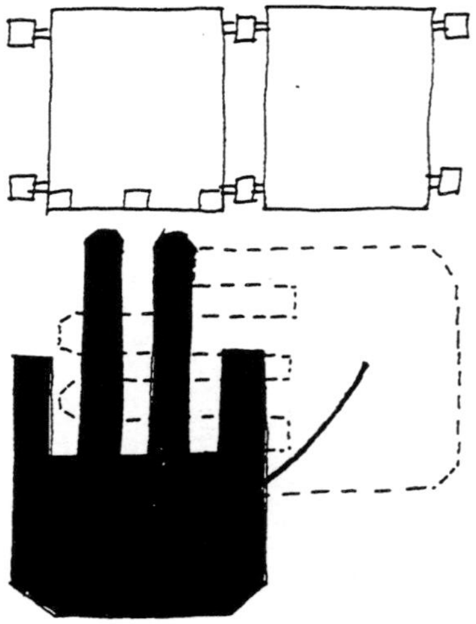

Swing into position facing the pallet.

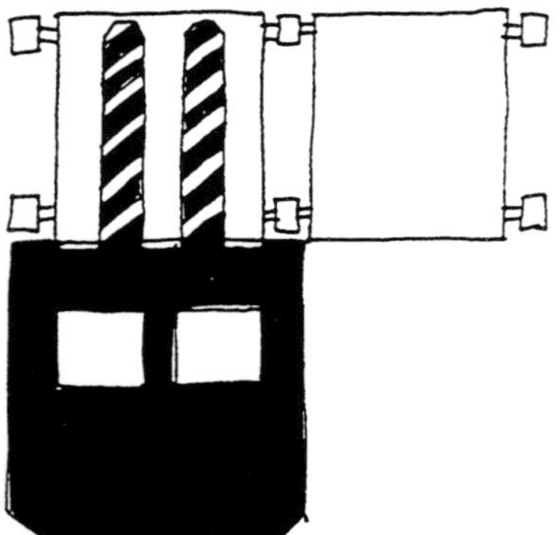

Extend the mast until the forks are completely under the pallet.

Lift the pallet about 5 cm. Tilt it backwards.

Raise your forks to the level of the required pallet.

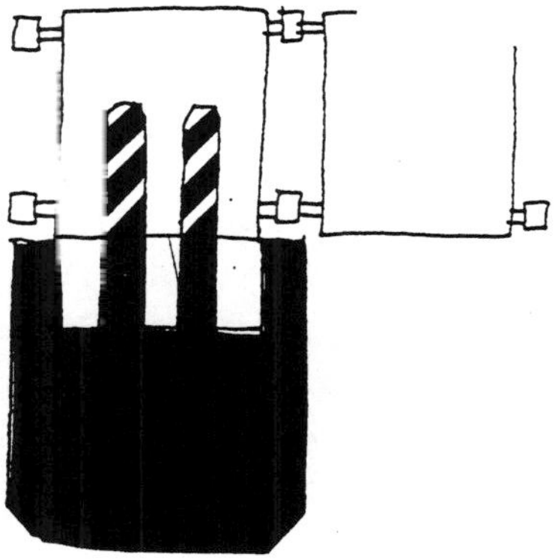

Drive forward so that the forks enter the pallet.

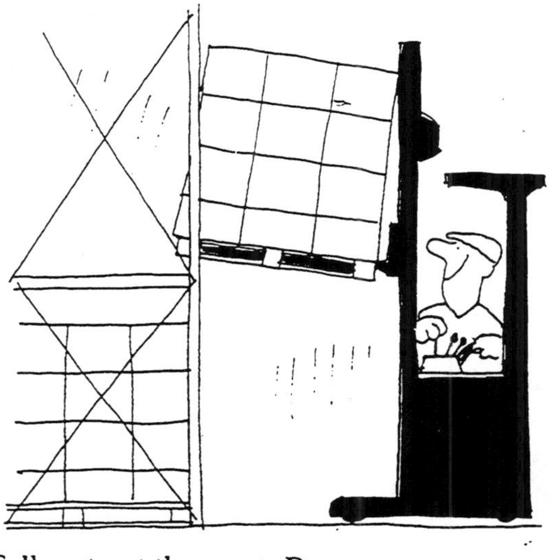

Fully retract the mast. Reverse to remove the pallet from the rack.

Lower the load to just above floor level. Swing back into your direction of travel.

Stand alongside the machine, raise the forks to the desired pallet.

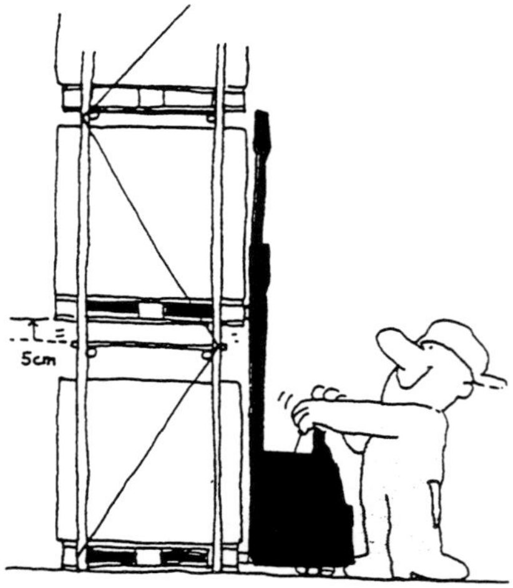

Move straight under the pallet, lift about 5 cm.

Back straight out, lower pallet.

Swing on full lock to travel position in aisle.

Chart and illustrations courtesy of **BT Rolatruc**

Fork Lift Truck - Stability - Inch Pound Rating:

Truck Ratings

Fork lift trucks are rated in terms of *the safe working load* in pounds or kilograms (***SWL***) that can be carried when the load is positioned with its centre of gravity at an ***SD*** - a stated distance in inches or centimetres , from the heel of the forks. In Ireland the ***SD*** is also known as the ***LC*** - Load Centre.

The correct way to describe an FLT is to quote both the SWL and the SD (LC).

A plate giving the rating must be fitted to each truck. If the truck is to handle loads of differing dimensions the plate should also give the safe loads for pertinent distances from the heel of the forks; for example 2500 kgs at 500mm.

This means that the truck is designed to carry safely a load of 2500 kgs (2.5 Metric tonnes) with a distance of 500mm between the centre of gravity of the load and the heal of the forks.

Caution must be taken when the truck is operating on uneven ground, as this can affect stability.

Fork Lift Truck - Motive Power Option:

Types of Power Unit:

1. *Battery electric*
2. *Diesel engine*
3. *Petrol engine (Very few in use. Supplied to special order)*
4. *Liquefied petroleum gas (LPG)*
5. *Duel Fuel - LPG/Petrol*

1. Battery Electric - Principal advantages

(a) Ideal for use inside factories / warehouses. Makes a minimum of noise, is clean in operation.
(b) Once daily maintenance schedule is followed the running cost is low, and the equipment has a long life.
(c) Has quick smooth acceleration.
(d) Works well under different weather conditions; e.g. no fuel to freeze.
(e) No waste of fuel while not working. No idling takes place; the engine is just switched off.
(f) Compact 24 volt and 48 volt battery electric three wheeler FLTs, with a clear view mast are available for narrow aisle work.
(g) The use of Superelastic tyres on medium sized wheels gives greater stability and extra height compaired to solid rubber tyres on small wheels.

Fork Lift Truck - Motive Power Option (continued)

Battery Electric - Disadvantages

(a) Speed is too slow for long distances.
(b) Requires special battery charging facilities, and procedures.
(c) Does not operate very effectively on steep inclines.
(d) Additional batteries are required for shift working. Night batteries are charged during the day.

2. Diesel - Principal advantages:

(a) High speed of operation for long distances, often over rough terrain.
(b) Being more robust than battery electric it can withstand severe operating conditions.
(c) Can be refuelled easily.
(d) Engine is reliable and has a long life; but, must be serviced as per manufacturer's instructions.
(e) Fuel can be stored in an over-ground tank.

Disadvantages

(a) Noisy in operation.
(b) Emits fumes which are objectionable but have low toxicity.
(c) Maintenance costs can be higher than battery electric if engine not adequately maintained.

3. Petrol Engine - Principal advantages

(a) Lower initial cost of the equipment.
(b) Can operate at high speed.
(c) Can withstand rough operating conditions.

Disadvantages

(a) Noisy in operation.
(b) Emits noxious (CO) carbon monoxide fumes.
(c) Maintenance costs are lower than for diesel engines. .
(d) Engine life depends on type of use ; e.g. 24 hour use (shift), or being used over rough terrain.
(e) Petrol storage requires; an expensive underground tank,and an expensive pumping system.

Fork Lift Truck - Motive Power Option (continued)

4. Liquefied Petroleum Gas (LPG) and 5. Dual Fuel Petrol/LPG - Principal advantages

Converted Petrol (high compression) engines can run on Petrol or LPG ("LPG", either propane or butane gas.)

(a) High octane rating of LPG allows the use of a high compression engine.
(b) LPG combustion is clean and complete even at idling speeds.
(c) Carbon monoxide (CO) in LPG exhaust fumes is less than that for petrol.
(d) With LPG, long engine life due to clean fuel.
(e) Spare Industrial Bottles of LPG can be stored in "lock-ups" made to an approved specification.
(f) Dual-Fuel engines can use petrol until the driver gets back to base for a gas bottle exchange.

Disadvantages

(a) Noisy in operation.
(b) LPG is both highly explosive and heavier than air and could, in the case of a leak, find its way into ducts, floor troughs and cellars. Adequate safety regulations must always be enforced. LPG trucks must not be parked in the vicinity of heaters, excavations, tunnels or cellars
(c) Most LPG trucks use bottles of gas, and both empty and spare full bottles must be kept under lock and key in a dedicated secure stock-yard structure.
(d) Managers must ensure that the complete LPG system is checked weekly.

Choice of the Power Unit:

Improved techniques in battery manufacture and pulse control systems for electric motors have increased the popularity of the Battery Electric truck for operations within buildings where the fumes and noise of Diesel, or Petrol trucks would be objectionable. LPG trucks can also be used internally and are an alternative to battery driven trucks where there are battery charging and changing problems; *unless the noise in use is a problem.* Fork lift trucks combine power travel with power stacking. Petrol only, combustion engine trucks, are seldom sold in Ireland today. Usually customer-choice is for dual-fuel models operating on LPG, with petrol as a back-up. Drivers often use petrol for a short while until they can install a new bottle of LPG. Soot filters and catalytic converters are available for FLTs, but their use is not compulsary under current Irish legislation.

Final choice of motive power will always depend on individual needs.

11 Logistics - Health and Safety Issues

Throughout this text, the reader will notice the frequency with which the word *Safety* occurs.
Safety and Packaging, Safety and the Package, Safety in the Stores, Good Housekeeping and the Stores, Fork-Lift Trucks and Safety; Safety and road vehicle Drivers, *and especially Materials Handling and Safety.* The list goes on and on. The word appears at every step of the supply chain.
Most Industrial (and Farm) accidents occur while movement is taking place. It is reasonable to say that "movement" activities ought to be carried out with great care.

Who is Responsible for Safety?

Legislation says that *Safety is everyone's responsibility.* We did not have to wait for legislation to say that; Common Sense has always told us so!

The Safety, Health and Welfare at Work Act, 1989 (which readers are advised to obtain and read in full), contains basic statements on safety in sections 6 and 9, which are summarized as follows:

Employers have a duty to ensure the health, safety, and welfare at work of all employees; while employees must take reasonable care for their own safety and that of any other person who may be affected. Employers must encourage and invite employees' views on health and safety matters, while employees must co-operate with the implementation of all statutory provisions of the Act.

Outside the legislation on health and safety issues, *employers may incur liability under Common law.* An employer must guard employees against any likely injury or disease *that is reasonably foreseeable.* The Courts have specified different elements of an employer's duty:

- Ensure plant and equipment are safe,
- Recruit competent workers,
- Provide protective equipment and clothing.
- Maintain premises in a reasonable state
- Ensure safe organization of work,
- Prevent employee-exposure to *avoidable* risks.

Correspondingly employees should use the protective equipment provided, (e.g. ear-muffs, shoes, overalls), and operate the approved machinery in a manner safe for all in their vicinity.

Safety Management Policy

The CEO of the company or a person specially appointed is responsible for co-ordinating safety matters, a task that is usually shared with other staff members.

Safety Management Involves the Following:	
Policy Formulation	***Design Procedures***
• *Identification of Hazards* • *Engineering Hazards Out* • *Instruction and Training* • *Personal Protective Equipment* • *Safe systems at Work* • *Review safety of Operations* • *Resources for Health and Safety*	• *Set up Regular Audits on Hazards* • *Eliminate dangerous components* • *Set-up relevant safety and first-aid programmes* • *Carryout Regular Audits* • *Develop good and unobtrusive supervision* • *Establish and use safety meetings* • *Use machinery guards and protective clothing*

<u>Materials Handling is a Key area for management attention to Safety</u>

12 Materials-Handling - Safety, Maintenance and Replacement

Industrial Trucks - Safety Rules:

Accidents with industrial trucks can occur through mechanical failure, illness or the physical unfitness of the operator. They can occur through the carelessness or laziness of the operator or others working in an area where FLTs are used. To minimise accidents resulting from carelessness, rules of conduct should be established and enforced through supervisors. Safety rules should be adequate, but realistic enough neither to restrict output without due reason, nor be too lax where there is an incentive payment scheme in operation. ***All personnel who come into contact with industrial equipment should be trained in safe operating procedures.***

Safety Rules for drivers of all Industrial Trucks:

1. Observe safe loading regulations.
2. Avoid sudden stops.
3. Watch for overhead clearances.
4. Ensure stability of load before proceeding.
5. Ensure stability of the load during transport.
6. Sound horn at junctions.
7. Avoid soft ground and damaged flooring
8. Take care at loading docks
9. Observe floor loading limits.
10. Travel slowly on gradients and on uneven surfaces with the load. Descend in reverse.

Special Safety Rules - for drivers of Fork, Reach & Order Picking Trucks:

1. Always face in the direction of travel.
2. Travel with masthead in a rearward tilt.
3. If the load inhibits forward vision, drivers should travel in a backwards direction.
4. Descend ramps backwards when truck is loaded - this should be avoided when the truck is not loaded.
5. Do not allow feet to protrude during operation.
6. Park with forks resting on the ground
7. Never allow a person to stand on raised forks, e.g. to count materials during a stock-take.
8. Forks should not be raised more than 8 inches, above the ground.
9. Swinging loads should be lifted only with proper attachments.
10. No vehicles of whatever type may be pushed with the fork-lift truck.
11. Never allow anyone to stand under the lifted load or to pass under the load.
12. Never carryout any maintenance or repair-work under lifted loads.
13. Never leave the fork-lift truck with the upright raised.
14. Check for gas leaks from LPG trucks.
15. Never participate in, or allow "joking" or "horseplay" on or near an FLT.

Safety Rules for Management - Use of Industrial Trucks

1. Allow only Qualified Drivers to operate trucks.
2. Encourage and enforce Pedestrian and Driver Discipline.
3. Prohibit the carrying of passengers.
4. ***Disallow smoking or naked lights near refuelling stations****. This applies no less importantly to battery electric trucks, because explosive vapours are given off during battery re-charging.*
5. ***Additionally, in the case of LPG trucks***, ensure that *the complete LPG system* is checked weekly to see that it is in an operationally safe state. Special attention must be paid to checking that the system is not leaking. For this use soapy water. When gas bottles need to be changed, *never* allow this to be done in inclosed rooms or garages. Ensure that those making the change always wear suitable gloves to prevent frostbite caused by evaporating liquid gas on the naked skin.
6. Enforce speed limits.
7. Install mirrors at blind corners
8. Incentives should be offered for accident-free driving; but schemes must be structured to discourage the hiding of any accident, whether imagined to be "*minor*" or otherwise.
9. Use colour schemes to indicate routes.

Remember . . . . Safety is Everybody's Responsibility!

Equipment - Maintenance and Replacement Policies are essential.
Modern Storage equipment systems are based on adjustable steel shelving, and variations of pallet racking. They are strong and long lasting. Materials-handling equipment, subject to much use and perhaps *abuse*, has a much shorter life and will need to be replaced in time.
The performance of manual and mechanical handling equipment, so essential to the smooth running of a stores, needs to be monitored on an on-going basis. The operating costs tend to increase with the life of the machine. *Two management policies will have to be employed: a Planned Maintenance Policy, and an Equipment Replacement Policy*

A Planned Maintenance Policy
A Planned Maintenance policy should ensure that the equipment will not break-down suddenly, causing panic in the department. Often called "Preventive Maintenance", Planned Maintenance is a systematic process of conducting regular checks on equipment to detect signs of wear and tear. Parts that are badly worn can then be replaced *before* they break down and cause major problems. Planned maintenance policies must be driven by the company CEO or MD. If left to operational managers to implement, many planned maintenance periods would be sacrificed when a machine has not actually broken down.

Equipment Replacement Policy - essential.
The Equipment Replacement Policy will permit Purchasing to source items and gather information on new products, well in advance of the time that the item does have to be replaced.. Just like our "next-door neighbours" in Marketing who use the *product life cycle* graph in determining when new products should be launched, we can plan the life of a machine on a graph to determine when a replacement machine is likely to be needed.

13 Automated Warehouses, Storage and Retrieval Systems

The benefits expected from the introduction of Automated Warehousing are:
1. Speedier service to customers.
2. Cost reductions in stockholdings.
3. Reduction in losses through pilferage, breakage and deterioration.

There are no completely Automated Warehouses; most are semi-automated. The level of human intervention, is in the area of Data Input. Japan leads the world in this technology; and in Europe the major user is Germany.
Automated Warehouses can operate around the clock, are fast and accurate, need fewer employees, and effect savings in lighting, heating, and ventilation.
An early example of Automated Warehousing is the Ford Warehouse in Dagenham. This warehouse, built in 1970, has 20,000 pallet positions and serves the assembly line alone. The total staff requirements are a Data Entry Clerk, Systems Analyst and, a "Trailer Un-Hooker".

Automated Warehousing - Components:

(A) A Controlling Computer

(B) Storage* and *Retrieval Machines (SRMs):

driverless FLTs
in-rack trolleys
stacker cranes

***(C) Storage Equipment*:**

small parts storage shelving and racking
carousels
high-bay racking

***(D) Input/output devices*:**

automated guided vehicles (AGVs)
conveyors

Automated Storage and Retrieval Systems AS/RS

The number of AS/RSs in the UK is less than 6% of the number in Japan. There are probably only four Irish companies using such systems. Excluding Germany, with 25% of the Japanese number, Europe has seen, only a modest growth, in numbers of AS/RSs, and AGVSs - automatic guided vehicle systems.

A bearing on these figures is that the systems are less flexible, and less easily modified, if so required.

Automated Warehousing may be considered when the following conditions prevail:

1. Manpower costs are high.
2. Storage in Unit Loads is possible.
3. Ability to issue materials in Unit Loads.
4. Product range has been reduced.
5. Consistent throughput, without major seasonal fluctuations.
6. Day and night shifts are in operation.
7. The existence of a product numbering system.
8. When space saving Random Stock Locations are prefered to dedicated Bin Locations.

AS/RS areas of mechanization within the Warehouse:

(a) Storage and retrieval Units for full pallets.

(b) High speed order picking equipment for cartons.

(c) Free Path picking machines. (Wire guidance systems).

(d) The "robotic" picking from either side of an aisle, using video camera vision guidance.

(e) Long load techniques -
 (i) Pigeon Hole racking with machine retrieval.
 (ii) Cantilever racking with stacker crane placement and retrieval.
 (iii) Cantilever racking with overhead Gantry devices.

Storage Equipment Choice

The efficiency of materials handling and the optimum use of warehouse space can be restricted by poor storage equipment. The orderly storage and handling of raw materials and finished products depends in large degree on the choice of suitable storage equipment. The choice of storage equipment depends on whatever permutation of relevant factors is appropiate for the stores function.

Factors to be considered include:

(a) value of the material(s)
(b) physical characteristics of the material/goods
(c) number of stock items
(d) forecasted rate of Stockturn*
(e) compatibility with existing storage equipment
(f) FIFO (First-in First-out) concept
(g) nature of the material - hazardous, contamination prone
(h) requirement for quick and convenient access to stock
(i) ease of physical counting
(j) general security

****Stockturn: Is the number of times in a period (e.g. a year), that a stock balance reaches or almost reaches a predetermined re-order level and is replaced with a new delivery. It can be calculated by dividing the value of the Material Issues in that period by the value of the Average Stock Holding.***

Typical Storage Eequipment Systems include:

(1) open shelving (used to store packaged items - screws, boxed components, containers of liquids such as grease, lubricants, paint)

(2) closed shelving (used to store packaged and loose materials - machine spares, hand tools, nuts and bolts, fuses, small components. Lockable doors can be provided for medical supplies, stationery items, and expensive items)

(3) bins

(4) outdoor platforms (to store e.g. 205 litre drums)

(5) pallets

(6) storage fixtures not classified as shelves or bins are called racks. The most popular racking is APR - *adjustable pallet racking*, which can be set out in single or back to back rows

(7) "drive-in" racking is used in many cold-store conditions to optimize expensive space and reduce refrigeration costs by blocking products together.

(8) carousels - a rotating device in which storage trays and bins can be brought to the operative by entering into the carousel keypad a row reference number. It is a space saving device that can accommodate goods of varying physical characteristics.

Loading Bays and Dock Equipment

Introduction

Loading bay procedures involve the movement of materials handling equipment, vehicles, and sometimes people, both inside and outside the building. Efficient administration on site is needed in coping with suppliers' and hauliers' drivers; employees and customers.

Loading-Bay efficiency is concerned with the following:

(1) the position of the bay or bays in the layout of the stores,

(2) the rate of issues from stocks,

(3) the frequency of deliveries to customers, and

(4) the transport vehicles used,

(5) the *right choice* of loading/unloading equipment used.

Choice of Equipment:

(a) FLTs, cranes, conveyors,

(b) devices for access to vehicles from ground level, ramps - fixed or mobile, loading platforms,

(c) mobile unit loads, roll-cage-pallets,

(d) VMLA (vehicle mounted loading-accessories), cranes, tail-lifts, fork-trucks; floor mounted conveyors.

14 The Unit Load Concept

Definition

The concept of the Unit Load is described as *"a quantity of materials, either in bulk or made-up of individual items, assembled, and where necessary restrained, to permit handling as a single object"*.

To get the greatest advantage from the Unit Load principle, it should be applied as far back in the supply chain or manufacturing cycle as possible, even to the raw material reception and storage stage. As the size of loads increases, the fewer are the journeys required to store a given quantity of materials.

The Advantages of Handling Goods in Unit Loads - Unitization:

"Materials handling economy is generally directionally proportional to the size of load handled"

(Stanley M. Weir, in "Order Selection" pp. 4-5. 1968)

(1) The likelihood of pilferage is greatly reduced.

(2) Handling of individual material items is reduced thereby lessening the possibility of damage.

(3) Outer packaging costs are reduced.

(4) In the palletizing of boxes and sacks, the criss-cross brick-like structure gives stability to the load.

(5) Efficiency of storage space is enhanced.

(6) Stock Control could be simplified if a full pallet is taken as the "unit of issue".

(7) Faster vehicle turn-around because loading and unloading time is reduced.

Unit Load methods

The main methods for Unit Loads are Pallets and Containers.

Pallets

Introduction

Pallets are platforms of wood, plastic, or other materials on which goods can be stacked to allow a bulk quantity to be relocated in one movement by an FLT, e.g. in the handling of cement, fertilizer, or bagged chemicals. Materials placed on pallets at the time of manufacture may so remain, for quite some time, until the first order quantity is required by a customer.

Structural foam moulded plastic pallets are now available, which combine low weight with high strength. Being easily washable, cross contamination is virtually eliminated. This advantage, together with that of its smooth top deck designed to eliminate all crevices that can harbour bacteria; has resulted in their growing popularity in the agriculture and food industry.

Pallets are usually classified as "two-way entry", "four-way entry" , "open-deck" or "closed-deck"; see drawings on following page.

Although Euro pallet sizes are 800mm. by 1200mm. and 1000mm. by 1200mm. there are still numbers of the original UK imperial measurement pallets being made.

Advantages of Pallets:

- Bulk quantities of the goods can be moved together and this reduces the manpower required for loading and unloading; thereby freeing labour for other stores work.
- Pallets facilitate the maximum use of storage space.

Disadvantages of Pallets:

- Goods not stacked properly on the pallet can easily be damaged.
- In the above situation, personnel can be seriously injured.
- In the stores, full pallets on full pallets may be stacked too high. Advice from the supplier of the goods should be sought.
- It is necessary to hire or buy an FLT to move the full pallets.

Pallets

Open Deck	Five Types
Closed Deck	Five Types

PALLETS

OPEN DECK

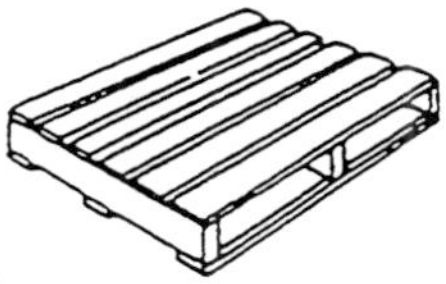

NON REVERSIBLE

CLOSED DECK

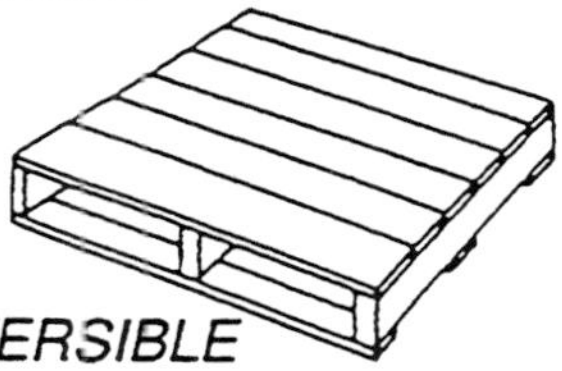

NON REVERSIBLE

OPEN DECK

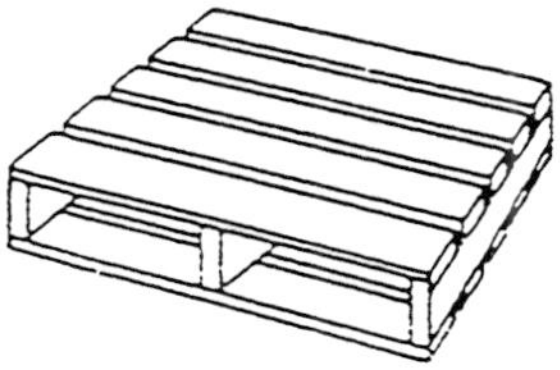

REVERSIBLE

CLOSED DECK

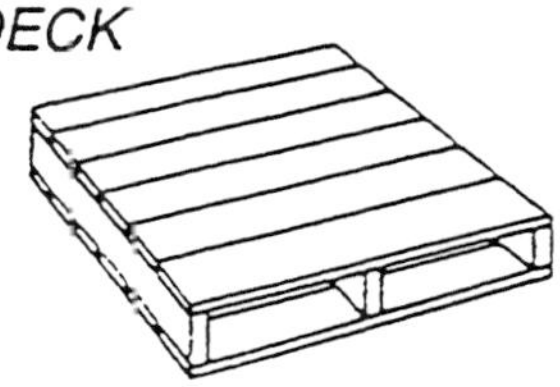

REVERSIBLE

OPEN DECK

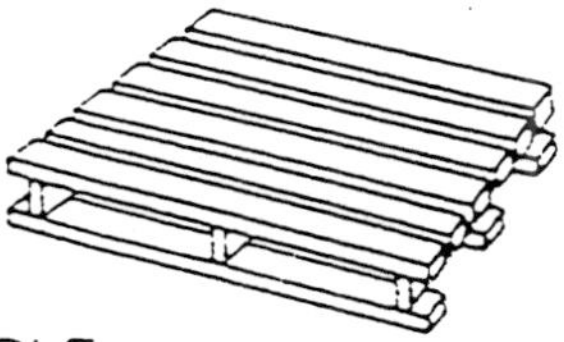

NON REVERSIBLE
WING TYPE

CLOSED DECK

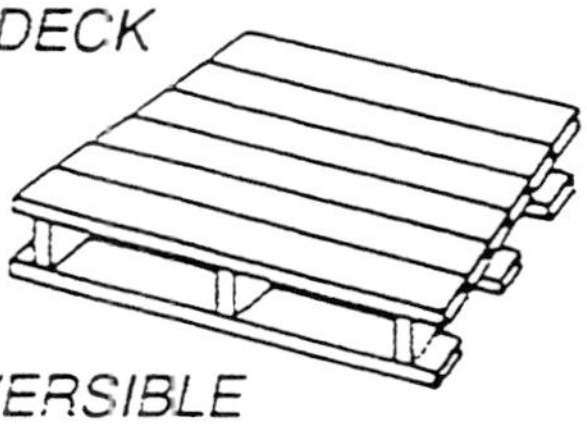

NON REVERSIBLE
WING TYPE

OPEN DECK

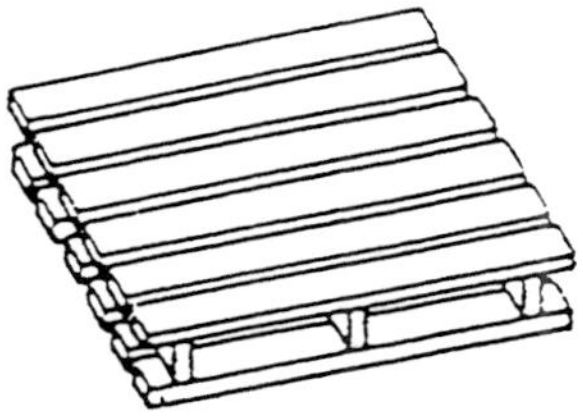

REVERSIBLE
WING TYPE

CLOSED DECK

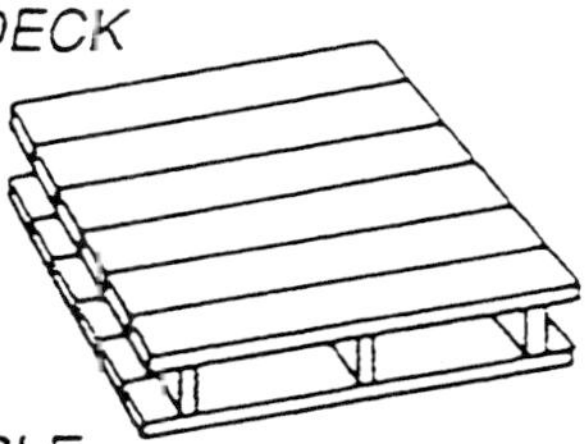

REVERSIBLE
WING TYPE

OPEN DECK

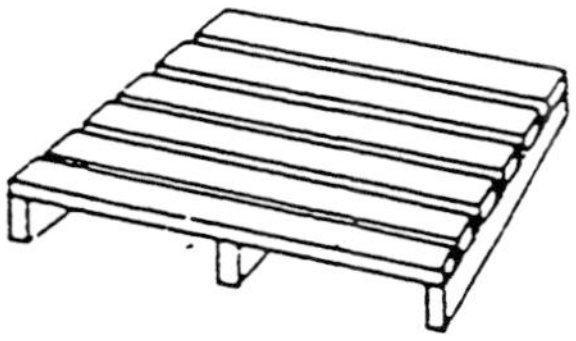

STILLAGE

CLOSED DECK

STILLAGE

Pallet Pool System

Originating in Australia, an idea to eliminate, or greatly reduce, the cost of transporting empty pallets over long distances, was developed into a practical system. The idea took some time to reach Europe; but once put into use, was an immediate success. It is a formal system of swapping pallets of pre-agreed dimensions, whereby loaded pallets received, are replaced immediately by empty ones; or exchanged within a specified time, e.g. 24 hrs. or 48 hrs.

The term "Pallet Pool" describes a process of pallet availability, provided by a company for its own use, or provided by a number of companies for their own use, in a logistics system. A "Pallet Pool" can also be provided by an independent service company, which can provide standard pallets on hire to manufacturers and distributors; who then become "*members*" of the pool.

In Ireland, many firms operate their own pallet pools and treat pallets as re-usable capital items; whilst many other firms use a pallet hire company. A well-known pallet-hire company operates a trans-European pallet pool with depots in most European countries including Ireland.
The main responsibility of control and repair lies with the pallet-hire company.

French and German railways have provided pallet pool systems, on a subscription basis for many years.

Some Advantages a Pallet Pool can offer members:

- The main advantage is that the uneconomic movement of pallets over long distances is virtually eliminated.
- Pallet administration by members is cut down considerably.
- Members, no longer have to budget for the purchase of pallets.
- Space problems in factories and warehouses are simplified because empty pallet stocks remain constant.
- Pool members need not worry about maintenance and replacement, because the cost is included in the hire or subscription charge.
- Senders and receivers of palletized goods, need only maintain a very small stock of pallets.

The Workings of the Pallet Pool System in mainland Europe

In Europe the pallet pool exchange method is employed. Members hand over empty pool pallets in exchange for loaded ones received. Exchanges are made between the Transport company and Senders, and between Consignees and Carriers. An exchange may be an immediate physical one, an exchange within an agreed specified period e.g. 24 to 48 hrs., or a net balancing exchange at agreed regular intervals. The last arrangement is usually confined to large numbers of pallets between adjacent transport systems.

In some pools, damaged pallets are repaired by the member in whose hands repair ultimately becomes necessary. A much more satisfactory and generally more economical system, is for a pool authority to effect repairs in its workshops, replace damaged pallets with good ones, covering its costs with the basic pool subscription.
Pool members may pay an annual charge based on the maximum number of pallets they dispatch in one day, or, as with the Dutch National Pool, an appropriate number of pallets is purchased from the pool authority. Membership is then renewable by further payments of the same amount, every three years

Containerization

Introduction

The container is now a fundamental feature of national and international transport modes, Road, Rail, Sea, and Air.

"Container" refers to *a standardized uniforn loading device* which is used to load goods.
Containerized materials in bulk can be moved from one mode to another - the inter-modal concept of transport. *The purpose of the container is to reduce the number of handling operations in freight transport.* The goods loaded into the container at the seller's premises, are checked, and the container sealed.

Containers are large *steel* boxes of standard sizes. They can be waterproofed and locked for security so that storage can take place in the open, saving warehouse space. Dimensions are approximately 8ft. high by 8ft. wide by a selection of lengths - 10ft., 20ft., 30ft., 40ft. 45ft not all common throughout the EU. Other materials are used in the construction of containers also; aluminium, plywood, or re-enforced plastic. Some containers for air-transport are specially shaped to the contours of the aircraft - these are called *igloos*. Special containers are available to carry specific loads, e.g. frozen food.

Legislation referring to the identification of containers are laid down in international standard ISO 6346 "Containers - Marking and Coding".

Containers

Standard 40ft.

Open-Top 40ft.

Flat-Rack 20ft.

Flat Rack Collapsible 40ft.

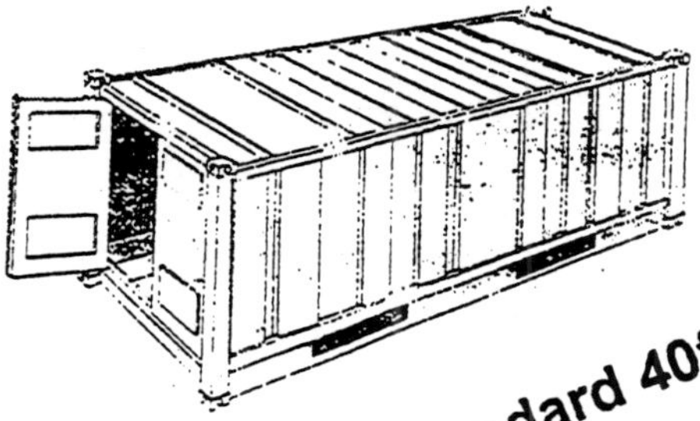

Standard 40ft.

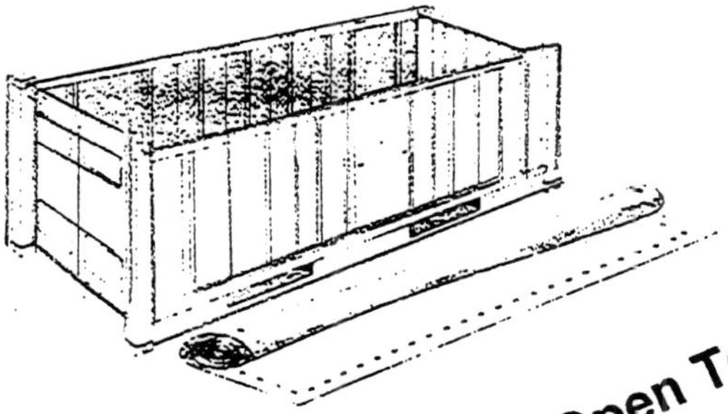

Open Top 40ft.

Flat-Rack 20ft.

Flat Rack Collapsible 40ft.

Groupage Containers

Containerised shipments may either be complete single shipments - FCLs (Full Container Loads) or, where shipments are insufficient in themselves to justify a full container, they may be brought together by a Forwarder or Carrier in an LCL (Less than Container Load) system. Forwarders' services of this kind are normally referred to as "Groupage" or "Consolidation".

There is a cost difference between carriers LCL. services and Groupage Services.

Containerization - Advantages and Disadvantages

Advantages

1. Improvements in labour productivity achieved.
2. Reduced handling time at Warehouse and at Docks.
3. Being sealed, they help to eliminate pilferage.
4. Possibility of damage to goods is considerably reduced.
5. Insurance costs are reduced.
6. There is the minimum of handling.
7. Available in a number of standard sizes.
8. Reduced need for packaging materials.
9. Handling costs at docks, and other terminals is reduced.
10. Reduced freight charges by material unit shipped.
11. Speedier clearance through international frontier posts
12. Service Levels, can be improved as all-round delivery time is faster.

Disadvantages

1. Initial cost may be prohibitive if the company wishes to own its own containers.
2. Cargo in uninsulated containers may be subjected to wide variations of temperature and humidity with the danger of mould growth and insect pest propagation.
3. Containers may leak, thereby causing damage from rain or sea-water.
4. The container may suffer from corrosion.
5. Cargo may be affected by the container position on ship, above or below deck.
6. Use of non-standardized pallets will cause loss of space in the container.
7. Metal and hard rimmed wheels on loading equipment can damage the floor of containers.
8. If the load in the container is not distributed evenly, problems in transit can ensue.
9. If the load is not arranged in such a way that unloading is simplified to suit personnel and mechanical equipment, accidents may occur.
10. Safety point. Empty containers previously used for the carriage of hazardous goods, must have a certific stating they have been cleaned and dried.

15 Purpose and Importance of an Efficient Transport System

An efficient system of transport is essential from the point of view of the manufacturer and the general public. The manufacturer, without a proper system, would have great difficulty in selling the finished products. Goods must, of course, reach the consumer to completely finish the sales process.
The manufacturer depends on transport in two ways:

1. To supply Raw Materials and Equipment for production.
2. To distribute the finished goods to the wholesaler, retailers and customers.

An efficient transport system, reduces the amount of capital tied-up in stocks - *the cost of storage* - by enabling replacement supplies to be obtained quickly. Lowering costs associated with purchasing and distribution, makes a direct contribution to the organization's profit.

Global Advantages and Disadvantages of an efficient Transport System

Advantages

- Countries are no longer isolated.
- Goods can be moved to areas of shortage from areas of surplus; i.e. famine relief operations.
- Peoples of different nationalities are brought into close contact with each other, thereby fostering friendship and understanding.
- Raw Materials are more easily exploited.
- New markets are opened up for manufacturers.
- The standard of living for people the world over, is improved.

Disadvantages

- Wealthy and powerful nations can more easily exploit the peoples of poorer and less educated nations.
- The speed and ease of modern transport to move the natural resources of these nations to other countries, allows no time for natural regeneration.
- By a combination of transport modes, foreign military powers can very quickly occupy overseas countries.

The Components of Transport:

There are three components:

The *"Unit of Carriage"* is the term used to describe the "thing" **in which** the people or the goods are being moved

e.g. railway goods wagons, lorries, and passenger carriages.
The efficiency of this unit depends upon its flexibility and adaptability

The *"Way"* is the term used to describe the route or "thing" **on which** the "Unit of Carriage " moves; e.g. natural ways like the open sea, air, pathways provided by nature, artificial ways like canals, railways, constructed road and motor-ways, and improved natural ways such as rivers, and harbours.

The "*Terminal*" is the term used to describe **a facility** where one mode of transport ends and another begins.
e.g. loading and unloading facilities at harbour-docks, airports, railway junctions.

The Elements of a Transport System:

There are three elements:

A "*Vehicle*" -in the widest sense of the word includes: buses and lorries, vessels of all kinds, and aircraft.

A "*Highway*" -again, in the widest meaning of the word, includes: roads, railways, sea and air.

A "*Terminal*" -as described above.

Six Essential Features of a Transport System including Cost

Efficiency and effectiveness of a transport system are determined by evaluating these factors:

(a) Cost,	*(b) Safety,*
(c) Speed	*(d) Convenience*
(e) Flexibility	*(f) Reliability*

(a) Cost:

Transport costs are directly related to distance travelled. This may deter a company from exporting to some foreign countries.

(b) Safety:

Vital with passenger transport. With goods, consignors must ensure goods are suitably packed and stacked to permit safe handling, loading and unloading.

(c) Speed:

Drugs, computer parts, production machine parts, perishable goods - airfreight in, as soon as possible. In these cases, cost is of less importance than speed.

(d) Convenience:

Ease to load and unload quickly and cheaply. Road may be more convenient than Rail.

(e) Flexibility:

Ability to carry large and small sizes of different types of goods.

(f) Reliability:

Raw materials must be received on time; deliveries to customers must be made on time. Freight collection delays lead to lost customers.

The Modes of Transport

There are several transport modes, which can be used to collect raw materials for a manufacturer or deliver the manufacturer's finished products to various channels of distribution. Choice of a mode depends on factors specific to each freight requirement. Those factors usually include decisions on *cost versus speed issues.*

Modal choice may favour one type, or a combination of two types. Fast transport can prove costly, and it is preferably used for light and perishable goods.

The Modes of Transport are:

(1) Road,
(2) Rail,
(3) Water - Inland and Sea,
(4) Air,
(5) Pipeline.

Transportation Modes - Selection, Change, Evaluation

An important responsibility of the manager in charge of Transport, is the selection of the most appropiate means of moving the organization's finished goods to the next point in the distribution network. This may be a delivery to a retailer, to a wholesaler, to a professional distribution company, or to an overseas agent. Often a direct delivery to a consumer or to an industrial end user, is made.

Although transportation costs in certain areas may reduce in the short time, due to local conditions, (e.g. the competition between P&O/Stena and the Eurotunnel); transport will continue to be a significant cost element in despatch and acquisition of materials.
It is not easy to ensure that choice of mode is at the one time, efficient, economical, and effective. Much information needs to be gathered and considered before the optimum choice of transport is possible. Information can be obtained from transport trade journals and directories.
Advice can be sought from members of CITI the Chartered Institute of Transport in Ireland.

Factors to be considered in selection

- Past experience with use of various transport modes.
  Is there a loss or damage history?
- Compatibility of the mode with the physical nature of the goods:
  e.g. delicate china or glassware; and hazardous chemicals.
- Other special characteristics of the product such as:
  perishability, security, or time constraints.
- Customer service needed:
  speed and reliability required,
  customer location, order/drop size, or any delivery constraints,
  can the mode deal with the frequency of, or modifications in, the service required by the organization?
- Is the mode to serve internal or external destinations.
- The need to balance cost with customer service;
  what are the relative costs of each transport mode?

16 Costs of Transport

Introduction

Costing means gathering together, recording and analysing all the relevant expenditures and revenues resulting from the purchase and operation of an asset; in this case a Transport facility.

Phase One
is the gathering information process.

Phase Two
consists of allocating and apportioning expenditures and revenues to each job or phase of operations as they arise.

Phase Three
is the expression of the various items as a cost and/or revenue per mile, kilometre, tonne, day, hour or other suitable standard; e.g. tonne-kilometer, which can then be applied to estimate the cost of individual jobs in the future.

The Objectives of Costing

(a) To provide managers with accurate information on the costs incurred in all areas of the service they provide, Road, Rail, Air, or Sea, etc., e.g. the running of Road vehicles, maintenance charges, staff costs, office overheads.

(b) To supply data on which to base policy.

(c) To provide cost estimates of future operations.

In order to achieve these Objectives efficiently -

* costs must be monitored
* every source of cost must be identified
* costs must be controlled to a predetermined plan.
* costs must be allocated in a consistent fashion

The Advantages of an Effective Costing System

* There is easy identification of profitable operations and activities.
* Relative profitability figures between different operations and activities are highlighted.
* Any areas of waste or loss should be clearly pinpointed.
* Information is available for: effective management planning and control, cost reduction exercises, and setting rates and charges.

Identification and Separation of Costs for Road Transport

In a road transport operation, total costs are made up of standing (fixed) costs, running costs (variable) and overhead costs. Some of the overhead costs are "fixed" and others are "variable". These costs can be separated and explained as follows:

RUNNING COSTS (direct costs / variable)	STANDING COSTS (fixed costs)	OVERHEADS (indirect costs: variable (v) or fixed (f))	
Fuel and Lubricants	***Licences (Excise & Operators)***	***Office Admin.***	***(f)***
Tyres	***Crew Costs***	***Postage***	***(v)***
Covers	***Vehicle Insurance***	***Telephone/Fax/EDI***	***(v)***
Overtime	***Interest on Capital***	***Advertizing***	***(f)***
Maintenance - Repairs	***Maintenance - Planned***	***Rent, Rates & Security on Premises***	***(f)***
	Depreciation or Leasing Charges	***Lighting, Heating, Ventilation and Insurance***	***(f)***

This allocation of costs is not rigid. For example, some operators consider maintenance charges,as distinct from repairs, to be a standing cost, and depreciation a running cost calculated on a cost per mile basis.

The decision on cost allocation rests with an individual operator. However, the end result should be much the same, provided the calculations are accurate and consistent.

Fixed

Standing Costs for Road Transport

Standing costs arise from being the owner or leasee of a vehicle. They are incurred whether or not the vehicle is running.

(a) Licences

This is the annual or quarterly duty to permit vehicles to operate on the public road. The tax is determined by:

(a) Unladen weight in the case of commercial goods vehicles.

(b) Seating capacity in the case of commercial passenger vehicles.

It also includes payments for operator's licences; and drivers' licences.

(b) Crew Costs

The basic wages of drivers are a fixed or standing cost, because they have to be paid whether the drivers are driving or not on a particular day and are not determined by drivers' output. Overtime payments should really be regarded as a variable or running cost.

Wages are not the only fixed cost associated with employing drivers. Other costs not connected with drivers' output are PRSI contributions, holiday pay, provision for pensions.

(c) Vehicle Insurance

The law demands that road vehicles be insured. In the case of a small fleet an insurance company will probably quote for individual vehicles. In the case of a large fleet where a blanket premium is paid some method of allocating insurance charges to individual vehicles must be agreed.

The insurance premiums discussed in this section refer to individual vehicles e.g. compulsory third party cover or comprehensive insurance.

Insurance of goods and passengers carried comes under "overheads".

[It is of use to mention here that a haulier does not insure the goods carried; a haulier's insurance is for coverage in the event of a claim for " goods damaged or lost through a haulier's ***negligence***"].

(d) Interest on Capital

Loans are usually repaid according to a fixed schedule. Repayments cover both the principal (i.e. the amount borrowed) and the interest.

Even if the money used to buy equipment comes from the operator's savings or from the firm's savings it still must not be regarded as "free" capital. By putting his/her own money into the business an operator is foregoing the interest that could have been earned by investing the money. The interest the operator foregoes is the opportunity cost of the capital.

Running Costs of Road Transport

(a) Fuel and Lubricants

Fuel charges are almost certainly the single most significant running cost and as such must be carefully controlled. Fuel costs can be recorded on a mileage, daily or even hourly basis for each vehicle.
Fuel consumption will vary according to the roads used, the loads carried and the driver's technique. By keeping a close check on fuel consumption an operator will be able to detect variations or discrepancies that may indicate maintenance problems.

(b) Tyres

The miles covered by each tyre during its useful life should be recorded so that pence per mile costs can be allocated. If properly kept and interpreted, records will give information on the best and safest type of tyre to use. Some large organizations lease tyres, e.g. Bus Áth Cliath.

(c) Covers

Covers are made from plastic material or from tarpaulin. The life of a cover, which depends more on the frequency of use and method of handling, than on bad weather, is often 2 - 4 years. Firms which sub-contract work to hauliers on a long term basis , often supply the covers and replacements free.

(d) Maintenance

This includes the cost of keeping the vehicle in a roadworthy condition capable of performing the tasks allocated to it. The recording of garage expenditure (where maintenance is carried out by the fleet owner) is a very difficult and complex operation. Because maintenance expenditure is a very high cost factor it is essential that every item of expenditure be recorded and subsequently related in an equitable fashion to the operation of individual vehicles.* This means, of course, that vehicles will be carrying the cost of garage rents and rates, lighting and heating, ancillary equipment, as well as the servicing and repair costs and labour.
The very diversity and complexity of operations in a garage raise special problems in recording the data and its subsequent allocation to vehicles for costing purposes. If the vehicles are maintained by outside garages, however, problems of cost allocation are considerably reduced.

Overheads

These are costs involved in running a business that cannot easily be allocated to a specific vehicle or a specific operation e.g. the cost of premises, telephone, postage, advertising, rates, salaries. and insurances.

***In the Republic of Ireland the cost of maintenance is higher than in the UK. The Irish cost has reduced slightly since 1995 due to the opening of new moror-ways; but it still is very high at almost 30% of running costs.**
This is mainly due to
(a). the smaller size of Irish companies means economies of scale are lost,
(b). parts are more expensive,
(c). vehicles are kept longer on the roads,
(d). lower standard of driving,
(e). poor road conditions.

Revenue and Expenditure are Equal

Break-even Analysis

Organizations differ from each other in the way they classify their transport expenses.
They also differ from each other in the *"cost unit"* they use, e.g. Tonne-kilometres, Packages, or Distance/kilometres.
The *break-even analysis technique* for identifying the minimum number of *"cost units"* which need to be sold before the transport organization begins to make a profit is a very important tool for the haulier; as it is for the company considering running their own fleet.
It is useful for the student to be aware of, and to be familiar with this technique. Rather than produce sets of figures for each of the *"cost units"* here is a simple example to explain break-even analysis.

As a member of your company's sports and social club you have been "volunteered" to organize the Christmas dinner dance. You have done your research and now want to know how many tickets need to be sold to cover all costs. Depending on the feasibility of this number, you will decide to run the dance or join in with a sister-company's function.
You list out the costs under the relevant headings - fixed or variable. Knowing that *fixed costs are those which remain the same regardless of the number attending*, e.g. the cost of the band, and *variable costs are those which are directly related to the numbers attending*, e.g. the hotel bill for the meal, you produce this chart.

Expense Heading	***Total IR£***	***Fixed Costs***	***Variable Cost per person***
Meal cost	20.00		20.00
Band or "Group"	150.00	150.00	
Bar Extension	87.00	87.00	
Glass of wine	2.50		2.50
Two Guests from US	45.00	45.00	
Printing Tickets	30.00	30.00	
Christmas Crackers	1.50		1.50
Totals:		312.00	24.00
Proposed Ticket price:	IR£ 30.00		

The Method: ***First***: Calculate, what our Accountancy friends call, the ***"Contribution"***,
i.e. *Selling Price per unit minus the Variable Cost per unit*
IR£30.00 minus IR£24.00 = IR£6.00

Then: Divide the ***Fixed Costs*** by the ***Contribution*** to get the ***Break-even figure***
IR£312.00 divided by IR£6.00 = 52

So if 52 people book and pay for tickets no loss (and no profit) is made.
For every ticket more than 52 sold, a profit of IR£6.00 is made.

Break-even analysis - is not too difficult to calculate, once fixed and variable costs are carefully identified.

17 Road Transport

Introduction

During the 18th century, the pathways made by our ancestors were turned into roadways and highways. The Industrial and Agricultural Revolution brought rapid expansion in output and development in all areas of commerce. To meet the needs of producers in distributing their goods, the quality of roadways was improved. The transport of goods by road is an important business sector in Ireland. Just over 100 million tonnes of goods are moved annually by road and rail; and the total work done is of the order of 5.25 billion tonne - kilometres.

Road is the dominant transport mode, taking over 95% of the total tonnes moved and undertaking almost 90% of tonne-kilometres performed. Ireland has seen a steady growth in road transport, since the early 1960s. This volume growth has initiated the construction of motorways, and continues to call for more, in the fight to reduce congestion and maintain adequate traffic flow.

Currently the Irish road network is a little over 90,000 kilometres.

The principal breakdown in the road haulage sector is between "Hire and Reward" and "Own Account". "Hire and Reward" operators are those who carry goods for others while "Own Account" operators are those who carry their own goods in their own vehicles. The reasons for the original large "Own Account" sector stem from the legislative provisions to which the industry was subject over the last 57 years. The "Own Account" sector, may not have been as tightly controlled in the earlier years as was the "Hire and Reward" sector. The proportion of work done by each group in Ireland is *estimated as follows*:

Main Use of Vehicle	1964 Tonne-Km millions (actual)	%	1994 Tonne-Km millions (actual)	%	1996 Tonne-Km millions (estimate)	%	1997 Tonne-Km millions (estimate)	%
Own Account	1.421	83%	1.846	35%	2.630	37%	2.950	36%
Hire or Reward	0.294	17%	3.412	65%	4.520	63%	5.250	64%
Total:	1.715	100 %	5.258	100%	7.160	100%	8.200	100%
Rate of Change			Gradual		Fast		Very Fast	

Road transport is the most commonly used mode in Europe

In the EU, the market for surface freight transport is very large. An estimate of the current total for surface freight movements within the Union is broken down roughly as follows:

Road	78%.
Rail	13%.
Inland waterways	9%.

In developing-countries, successful implementation of Government policy, depends to a great extent on the quality of transport modes within their territories; road transport being the most important.

Road Transport - Advantages and Disadvantages

Advantages

1. Can provide a door to door service.
2. Physical handling is reduced because of the need to load and unload only once.
3. Each part of the country is accessible by lorry.
4. Transportation by road can be achieved 24 hours a day.
5. For the short journey, road transport is the fastest.
6. Suitable for fast direct delivery of perishable goods.
7. Can be relied upon to provide connecting services to other transport modes.
8. If the carrier or owner arranges for return loads the cost of transporting can be reduced.
9. The flexibility of road transport is such that changes can be made relatively easily.
10. ESTC - Electronic Satellite Tracking & Control systems improve Long Haul delivery time and flexibility. TNT, DHL - Cab   Security, location
11. On-going construction of motorways up to EU stds., reduce congestion, and permit faster runs.

Disadvantages

1. The speed of delivery can be slowed down considerably because of traffic jams.
2. Can be affected by adverse weather conditions.
3. Large lorries require a minimum of two people, generating extra cost for larger consignments. Safety
4. Large lorries cannot use narrow roadways.
5. The transportation of large items of machinery requires detailed planning and assistance from the local authorities. Movement of ESB pylons is an example, *but there may be no other suitable mode to use!* New foot bridge from Centre to Dublin
6. Low bridges often cause diversions and sometimes damage to the load being carried.
7. The geographical location of the customer, even within the supplier's own country, can increase the delivery time because of speed restrictions imposed by the local authorities.
8. Environmental damage - the narrow view, i.e. to historic old buildings, and crops. Some cities even prohibit passage through their streets, and diversions and delays are inevitable.
9. Environmental damage - the broader view; we can expect increasing restrictive legislation because: *exhaust fumes from petrol and diesel engines produce over 20% of the oxides of nitrogen that are causing "acid rain". road transport produces up to 40% of the SPM (suspended particulate matter/smoke) which is recognized as a cause of respiratory ailments.* (UK figures, no Irish figures available to hand).

   However, new technology, e.g. the use of catalytic converters reduces the level of Carbon Monoxide (CO) emissions.
10. European long distance vehicle drivers can cause almost instantaneous disruption in countries by setting up road blockades, as part of their industrial action. The French drivers' policy is *"prevent the population at large from getting supplies of bread and petrol; then we will get what we want"*. Irish hauliers have been seriously affected by these blockades. Irish manufacturers could stand to loose millions of pounds, each time there is a strike.

Vehicle Selection - Heavy Goods Units, and Vans; Light Commercials:

Heavy Goods Units:

Goods Units fall into two broad categories, *Rigid and Articulated*

1 Rigid

These units embody the propulsion unit and the *unit of carriage* in a single vehicle.
Rigid Vehicles having greater stability and road holding qualities, give greater safety margins..
Rigid Vehicles are capable of towing *two-axle or three-axel "Draw-bar-trailers"*.
Towing equipment used with rigid units is designed with a high degree of safety in mind.
Such equipment includes: Towing Jaws, Towing Hooks, Self Aligning Corner Stays (used to strengthen the towing member).
There are some applications in which Rigid Vehicles are preferred to Articulated vehicles, viz: off-the-road work, and site work, where the stability of the unit is far superior and safer.

2 Articulated

This type of vehicle comprises a *Tractor unit and a separate Trailer unit for goods,* which are coupled together. The Tractor unit has a short chassis and normally consists of four or six wheels. The trailer units can have one, two or three axles with either single or double wheels and have retractable wheels on which the front end can be supported when it is detached from the tractor unit.

The Advantages of the Articulated unit over the Rigid unit:

Articulated units are more manoeuvrable than Rigid units especially in their "Turning Circle". They are more economical to use than Rigids; one advantage being that a number of trailer units can be used with one tractor unit (not all together, of course)!

1. Facilitates interchange of Goods Units.
2. Economic use of driver's time.
3. Increased manoeuvrability. (Turning circle).

However, there is a danger of jack-knifing, trailer swing and overturning

Vans and Light Commercials - Features:

1. 7 cwt (vans) to 3 tons (light commercial)
2. Require normal "C" Licence only to operate
3. Used in city environment for door to door deliveries
4. Body usually of welded steel with large rear doors for loading and unloading.
5. Power unit can be Diesel or Petrol (4 Cylinder)
6. Some Light Commercials have a rear pull-down step and roller shutter type doors.

Sub-classification of Goods Units:

(a)	Covered Vans	(d)	Open Trucks
(b)	Tippers	(e)	Platform Vehicles
(c)	Tankers	(f)	Hopper Vehicles.

There are many more types of goods units. Many of them include attachments to assist with loading and unloading.

The Three Stages of Vehicle Procurement

1. Carryout a Feasibility Study

Before attempting to acquire even one vehicle, the transport manager and the company buyer will carryout a suitable survey or feasibility study on the following:

(a) why the vehicle(s) are wanted in the first place
(b) type of vehicle; Van, Rigid truck, or Artic.
(c) types of load, and any special characteristics
(d) main types of vehicle body
(e) the size of vehicle
(f) annual mileage to be covered
(g) the engine type
(h) required working life of the vehicle
(i) identify relevant vehicle suppliers
(j) compare prices of various makes, *and then*
(k) assess actual fleet requirements

.2. Assessing Fleet Requirements

Road Hauliers and Transport managers must give very careful thought and consideration to the number of vehicles required for the company, to their size, shape and capacity.

In assessing the number of vehicles required it is useful to have consignment records for each week of the year. Thus, peak and valley weeks will be shown quite readily and also the extent to which the demand is likely to fluctuate. The cost of catering for peak requirements can be very expensive if the peak lasts only a few weeks. The question must then be asked as to whether one's own transport will cater for all requirements. If the answer is 'No!", and *partial sub-contracting* is not a serious consideration, then an extra vehicle(s) will need to be procured.

Suitability of a particular Vehicle Type

As a general rule it can be stated that the most economical costs per unit carried, can be achieved with the largest vehicle available. However, even if a distributor has sufficient volumes of goods to fill large vehicles, it may not be practicable to operate them for one or more of the following reasons.

1. Poor access or space limitation problems at customers' premises,
2 The pattern of distribution, e.g. small consignments, would make large vehicles both uneconomical and unsuitable.

In deciding, therefore, on the size of the vehicle, critical questions must be asked about:

(1) the value of goods to be distributed,
(2) the delivery pattern and number of drops,
(3) the physical constraints on maximum size because of access and space constraints at loading and unloading points.

Road Transport Vehicles

Light Van

Medium Van

Light Four-Wheeled Rigid Vehicle with Box-Van Body

Rigid Vehicle with Draw-Bar Trailer

Articulated Vehicle Tractive Unit and Semi-Trailer

LIGHT VAN

MEDIUM VAN

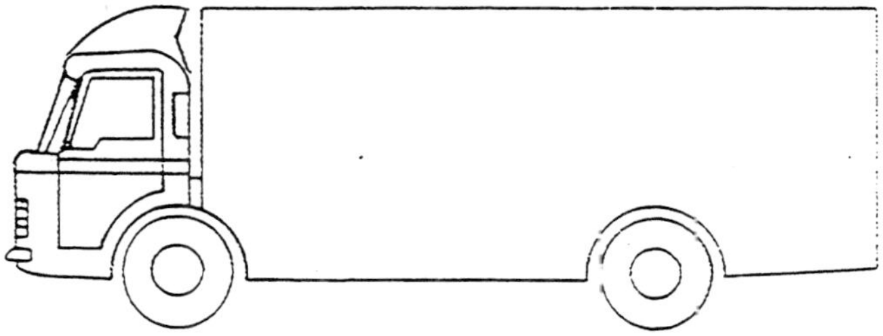

LIGHT FOUR WHEELED RIGID
VEHICLE WITH BOX VAN BODY

RIGID VEHICLE WITH DRAW BAR TRAILER

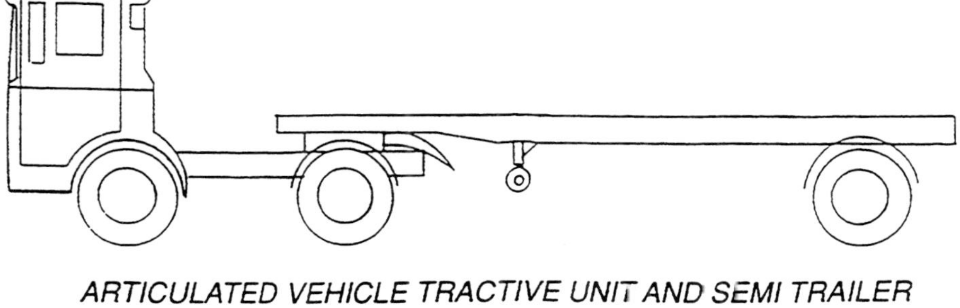

ARTICULATED VEHICLE TRACTIVE UNIT AND SEMI TRAILER

3. Vehicle Acquisition

There are three or four options open to the Buyer and Transport Manager.

Outright Purchase: The vehicle belongs to the operator, and with proper maintenance, it should have a good trade-in value when it needs to be replaced.. Suitable when a firm's cash-flow can cope well with large payment(s)

Hire Purchase: The operator has use of the vehicle without having to buy it. Responsibility for comprehensive insurance, road tax, and maintenance is with the hirer. Besides the monthly payment, the firm's cash-flow is not affected. When the last payment is made, title in the vehicle passes to the hirer. Under the 1946 Hire-Purchase act, after the first three months' payments have been made, there are safeguards for the hirer over the balance of the contract period.

Leasing: The vehicle always belongs to the leasing company, but the lessee has full use of the vehicle. Again, responsibility for comprehensive insurance, and maintenance is with the lessee. The vehicle cannot be returned to the leasing company, before the end of the contract, without a penalty. There is no capital commitment; cash flow is not affected by other than a monthly lease-hire charge.

Hiring: The vehicle remains the property of the rental company, which retains responsibility for maintenance and road tax. Usually comprehensive insurance must be provided by the hirer. No capital commitment is called for; and the vehicle(s) can be returned at any time.

Best Option: For a cash-rich company, it is of course outright purchase; for other companies, *leasing* has many advantages.

The Importance of Maintenance

Important from three viewpoints

1. *From the point of view of customer service.* Just as with a private car, everything is fine with a transport vehicle until there is a breakdown. A private car breakdown is one thing, but breakdown of a transport vehicle can cause immense problems. Loads may have to be transferred to another vehicle, which may not be readily available. Urgent orders for customers will be delayed, which in some circumstances could lead to the loss of that customer.

Delays of intermodal transfers are costly, and time lost in a particular case is not recoverable.

2. *From the safety viewpoint.* Statistics show that many accidents are caused directly by technical defects, including bad lighting, and defective steering. Again, statistics show that vehicles not maintained in suitable condition contribute to non-technical accidents, caused by carelessness, lack of concentration, and bad weather.

3. *From an economics viewpoint.* Keeping a vehicle in proper condition gives longer vehicle life, a better performance, and in general, saves money.

A proper maintenance policy, must include a planned element. Planned Maintenance, has its roots in the idea of "Prevention is better than Cure". It develops confidence of both staff and customers, in the organization's ability to perform to the highest quality standards.

Maintenance consists of the following activities:

(a) *Planned Maintenance* is the management task of identifying certain equipment and key parts of that equipment, and by systematic monitoring at predetermined times, to check for warning signs of impending failure,and to take corrective action if necessary.

(b) *Servicing* is a routine activity carried out at the intervals suggested by the manufacturer of a vehicle, or other equipment, e.g. oil changes, lubrication, and oil filter change. Other faults discovered during the servicing can also be put right.

(C) *Breakdown repairs* when components malfunction during use. Speedy attention is essential.

(D) *Planned Repairs* necessitates:

(1) the listing out of those items identified by a manufacturer as needing attention, or replacement after a specific time period or miles travelled,

(2) keeping records of repair / replacement due-dates, and

(3) carrying out the instructions of the manufacturer, accurately to ensure no interruption to vehicle availability.

Maintenance - Summary

It is vital that maintenance is carried out without reducing the effectiveness of the vehicle fleet. It is important that drivers are properly trained in the use of new vehicles, as bad driving habits learned in other jobs or in using other vehicles, can lead to breakdowns, or worse!

Vehicle Replacement Policy

Maintenance charges substantially increase towards the end of the effective life of a vehicle. Fuel economy reduces as the vehicle's working life draws nearer to its end. As with maintenance, a systematic programme of evaluating the required benefits from a vehicle is important; because requirements change over time. Regardless of maintenance costs, there are a number of factors that lead an organization to consider replacing a vehicle.

1. A newer or better model is now available,
2. Scarcity of parts is a major maintenance problem,
3. Load characteristics have changed,
4. The market's geographical area has increased,
5. To compete with the Image of the competition, Marketing
6. Required as part of a revised policy on improving customer order cycle time.

General Design Features of Modern Vehicles to be considered

A. City Work

In relation to different types of operation, the following are the main points for consideration:

- manoeuvrability
- good turning circle
- generous and regular shaped cargo-areas, with few intrusions
- large and wide-opening rear doors
- good all-round vision from cab
- easy assess for driver
- comfortable location of foot-pedals to minimise clutch and braking wear
- general cab comfort.

B. Long-Haul Journeys

Along with the above, consider also:

- payload
- mechanical efficiency
- fuel consumption
- overall journey performance.

Vehicle Routeing - Route Planning, and Vehicle Scheduling

The Vehicle Routeing Objective: To reduce transport costs while improving customer service. The two variables in *Vehicle Routeing* are *distance travelled* and *time taken.*

Route Planning and Vehicle Scheduling address the task of identifying the best paths through which a vehicle should travel to minimize length of journey or/and time taken.

There are two basic ways used to effect the optimum use of vehicles.

1. Ensure that the vehicle is working as long as possible. Some taxi owners work for 12 hours and a hired driver takes over for the next 12 hours.

2. Ensure that vehicles are loaded to full capacity.

By *planning routes, vehicle loads and delivery timings,* an operator can control and improve productivity; however there are a number of constraints that must be considered.

Capabilities - Vehicles	*Capabilities - Drivers*
Load Size and Weight	*Limitation of Time Available per day*
Loading and Unloading Access Times	*Knowledge and Experience of Routes*
Running Speeds	*Physical Ability*
Operating Costs, e.g. Leasing	*Reliability*
Traffic Congestion	*Problem Solving Ability*

18 Driving - EU Regulations

Guide to EU Council Regulation No. 3820/85 on Drivers' Hours and Rest Periods and EU Council Regulation No. 3821/85 on The Tachograph. Additional information for references purposes only is given in appendix 1.

Introduction

This ***guide*** is intended to give a convenient outline of the principal provisions of EU Regulations No. 3820/85 on *drivers' hours and rest periods* and EU Regulation No. 3821/85 on the *Tachograph* and on the statutory instruments which implement these Regulations in this country. ***The information given is not exhaustive, and is not intended to be an authoritative legal interpretation. Where necessary, the EU Regulations and Statutory Instruments should be consulted.***

Purpose of the EU Regulations:

The purpose of the *Tachograph* regulation, is to ensure that drivers will adhere to the regulations on drivers' hours, breaks, and rest periods. The purpose of those regulations have their origin in the reaction to the horrific accidents on European motor-ways, caused by drivers falling asleep while in control of their vehicles; killing themselves and innocent motorists. For a number of wrong reasons, either on the part of the drivers themselves, or the vehicle owners, drivers were driving continuously for long numbers of hours without adequate rest.

Since the implementation of the regulations, accident numbers have declined whilst vehicle traffic has increased.

Many lives have been saved as a result of these regulations.

Definitions: In the EU Regulations, words and expressions have been defined as follows:

(a) "*Carriage by road*" means any journey, made on roads open to the public, of a vehicle, whether laden or not, used for the carriage of passengers or goods;
"Vehicles" means motor vehicles, tractors, trailers and semi-trailers, defined as follows:
"Motor Vehicle": any mechanically self-propelled vehicle circulating on the road, other than a vehicle running on rails, and normally used for carrying passengers or goods.
-"Trailer": any vehicle designed to be coupled to a motor vehicle or a tractor.

(b) "*Driver*" means any person who drives the vehicle even for a short period, or who is carried in the vehicle in order to be available for driving if necessary.

(c) "*Week*" means the period between 00.00 hours on Monday and 24.00 hours on Sunday.

(d) "*Rest*" means any uninterrupted period of at least one hour during which the driver may freely dispose of his time.

Driving Periods, Breaks, and Rest Periods

The Drivers' Hours EU Regulation 3820/85 *applies to drivers of vehicles that have a permissible maximum weight over 3.5 tons, which in Irish law is deemed to be 1524 kilograms (1.5 metric tonnes) unladen weight. This regulation covers any journey or part of a journey made within the EU.*
(For the recor, one ton = 2,240lb, and one tonne = 1,000 kilograms or one metric tonne.)

Breaks from Driving: The maximum period of driving without a break is 4.5 hours, after which a break of at least 45 minutes must be taken. This break may be replaced by three shorter breaks of 15 minutes each, distributed over the driving period or immediately after it, in such a way that a cumulative break of at least 45 minutes has been taken after the 4.5 hours driving.

During a break the driver may not carry out any other work. However, waiting time and time not devoted to driving, spent in a vehicle in motion, a ferry or a train, will not be regarded as other work. The 4.5 hours relates to driving only and does not include other work.

Daily Driving Period:

The preferred maximum period recommended under EU Regulation 3820/85 is 9 hours , however, this may be extended to 10 hours, but not more than twice in any one week. The definition of a daily driving period is the driving period between any two daily rest periods or between a daily rest period and a weekly rest period.

Fortnightly Driving:

The total period of driving in any one fortnight must not exceed 90 hours.

e.g. week one 56 hrs. ((4 @ 9) + (2 @ 10))
week two 34 hrs. (90 - 56)

Daily Rest Period:

In each period of 24 hours, the driver must have a daily rest of at least 11 consecutive hours.
If the driver needs to split the rest period into two or three parts, one part must be of 8 hrs. duration, *and* the driver must increase the 11 hrs. to 12 hrs.

This daily rest of 11 consecutive hrs, may be reduced to 9 consecutive hours, on three days (only) in any one week, *provided:*

(a) the shortfall figure will be made up ***by the end of the following week***, and

(b) this shortfall figure will be added to a rest period of ***at least, 8 hrs duration.***

Where a vehicle is staffed by two drivers, each driver must have a rest period of not less than 8 consecutive hours during each period of 30 hours. (Note, not 24 hrs !) The daily rest period may be taken in the vehicle provided it is fitted with a bunk and is *stationary.*

.Rest periods may not be taken on a moving vehicle.

There are some specific exemptions to these rules, including one in relation to Ferry crossings; which we will describe now, as it has a bearing on the value, or otherwise, of the Channel Tunnel to Irish drivers; an important consideration covered later in this text.

Daily Rest Period and Ferry crossings:

To accommodate a ferry crossing, a daily rest period can be split into two parts; one part of which must ***be taken on board the ferry***. The other part, ***taken on land***, can take place, either before or after the crossing.

The part taken on land ***must be finished within a maximum of one hour***, either *before or after* the part taken on board the ferry. Time spent on customs facilities, must be *included* within this hour.

The driver must have access to a bunk or couchette during both portions of the rest period.

Where the daily rest period is split in this way, it must be increased to 13 hours.

Weekly Rest

A week is defined as the period between 00.00 hours on Monday and 24.00 hours on Sunday.

During each week, a daily rest period must be extended into a weekly rest period totalling 45 consecutive hours. This may be reduced to 36 or 24 consecutive hours under certain circumstances.

A weekly rest period must be taken after no more than six daily periods.

Emergencies

A driver may depart from the provisions of the Regulations on drivers' hours, to enable him to reach a suitable stopping place, to the extent necessary to ensure the safety of persons, of the vehicle or its load. The driver must indicate on his Tachograph chart or duty roster the nature of the departure from the Regulation with the reason.

Drivers' Duties

Drivers must comply with the provisions of the EU regulations 3820/85 and 3821/85.

(a) Use record sheets every day they are driving.
(b) There must be separate Tachograph charts (discs) for *each* driver of a vehicle, for *each* day.
(c) Record sheets must not be used for longer than the period intended.
(d) Not use soiled or damaged sheets.
(e) Make, or cause to be made, an entry on ,or alteration to any record sheet ,which entry or alteration, they know to be false.
(f) Interfere with the Tachograph in any way, for any reason whatsoever.
(g) Record sheets must be returned to the employer for inspection and retention, within 21 days.
(h) Drivers must be able to produce record sheets and Tachograph charts (discs) for the current week and for the last day of the previous week on which they drove, when requested to do so by an inspecting officer.

SUMMARY OF DRIVERS'S HOURS REQUIREMENTS - EU REGULATION No.3820/85

FOR NATIONAL AND INTERNATIONAL OPERATIONS

Subject	*Goods Vehicles*	*Passenger Vehicles*
Daily Driving (Total)	9 hours (10 hours twice a week)	Same
Total Driving Time without a break	4.5 hours	Same
Breaks from Driving	45 minutes (which may be divided into breaks of at least 15 minutes each distributed over the driving period or immediately after it)	Same
Weekly Driving (Maximum)	56 hours (six daily driving periods - 4x9 + 2x10)	Regular services - 56 hours (six daily driving periods) Non-regular services - None
Fortnightly Driving (Maximum)	90 hours total One week 56 hrs, other week 34 hrs	Regular services - 90 hours Non-regular services - 112 hours (Twelve daily driving periods)
Daily Rest - One Driver	11 hours reducible to 9 hours three times a week (subject to compensation) or 12 hours split into 8 hours + one or two other periods	Same

Subject	Goods Vehicles	Passenger Vehicles
Daily Rest - One Driver (continued) Ferry Crossings	13 hours split into two periods 8 hours (minimum) + the balance, one period of which must be taken on land before or after sailing. Time between periods to be not more than one hour including customs formalities	Same
Daily Rest - Two Drivers	8 hours in each 30 hour period	Same
Weekly Rest	45 hours reducible to 36 (at base) or 24 (away) from base subject to compensation	Regular services - 45 hours reducible to 36 (at base) or 24 (away from base) subject to compensation Non-regular services - 90 hours (after 12 daily driving periods)
Week EU Definition)	Fixed - 00.00 hours Monday to 24.00 hours Sunday	Same

NB. This chart is intended as a general summary only, to assist students. For complete details please consult the regulations.

Enforcement

It is an offence for any person to contravene or cause or permit any person employed by him to contravene any provision of the Regulations. In the event of prosecution fines up to IR£1,000 or six months imprisonment or both may be imposed.

In the Republic of Ireland, the officers empowered to enforce the requirements of the EU legislation are:

(1) Transport Officers, persons appointed by the Minister for Public Enterprise,

(2) any Customs and Excise officer,

(3) any member of the Gárda Síochána.

Employers' Duties

(1) General duties - a selection:

Employers must comply with the provisions of the EU regulations 3820/85 and 3821/85.

(a) Organize drivers' work in such a way that drivers are able to comply with these relevant provisions.

(b) Make periodic checks to ensure that these EU provisions are being complied with, and to take corrective action if infringements are detected.

(c) Ensure that drivers have a sufficient number of sheets and Tachograph charts (discs), approved for the instrument in the vehicle.

(d) Keep records in a suitable manner, enabling checking by an authorized inspecting officer; and enabling copies to be issued to drivers requesting them.

(e) Make, or cause to be made, an entry on ,or alteration to any record sheet ,which entry or alteration, they know to be false.

(f) Interfere with the Tachograph in any way, for any reason whatsoever.

(g) Comply with verbal and written requests, from an authorized inspecting officer, for the purpose of checking compliance with the provisions of the EU and Irish Regulations.

(2) Specific: Payments

Payments, even in the form of bonuses or wage supplements, related to distances travelled and/or the amount of goods carried are *not* allowed; *unless* they are of such a kind as not to endanger road safety.

The EU Regulations apply to carriage by road, by:

(a) Goods Vehicles over 3.5 tons maximum permissible weight which in Irish law is deemed to be 1524 kilograms (1.5 Metric tonnes) unladen weight.

(b) Passenger Vehicles constructed and equipped to carry more than nine persons including the driver.
However, passenger vehicles on regular national passenger services where the route covered by the service in question exceeds 50 kilometres (31 miles) are exempted from use of the Tachograph but not from the drivers' hours requirements. *In such an instance, a service timetable and a duty roster must be drawn up by the operator;*

(c) Passenger vehicles on regular international passenger services, whose route length does not exceed 100 kilometres, have been subject to Tachograph regulations since 1st January 1990. (Timetables and duty rosters were acceptable previous to that date.)

Exemptions

There are a number of exemptions from the EU regulations; some of which are:

(1) Vehicles used for the carriage of goods where the maximum permissible weight of the vehicle, including any trailer or semi-trailer, does not exceed 3.5 tons, - 1.5 tonnes.
(2) Vehicles with a maximum authorised speed not exceeding 30 kilometres per hour.
(3) Vehicles used by or under the control of the armed services, civil defence, fire service, and forces responsible for maintaining public order.
(4) Specialised breakdown vehicles.
(5) Vehicles used in emergencies or rescue operations.
(6) Vehicles used in connection with the sewerage, flood protection, water, gas and electricity services, highway maintenance and control, refuse collection and disposal, telegraph and telephone services, carriage of postal articles, radio and television broadcasting and vehicles. used in the detection of radio or television transmitters or receivers. Essential Services
(7) Vehicles transporting circus and fun-fair equipment.
(8) Vehicles used for non-commercial carriage of goods for personal use. Moving furniture
(9) Tractors used exclusively for agricultural and forestry work.
(10) Vehicles used for milk collection from farms and the return to farms of milk containers or milk products intended for animal feed.
(11) Vehicles used for driving instruction with a view to obtaining a driving licence, provided a vehicle so used or any trailer or semi-trailer drawn by it, is not carrying out a journey in connection with the carriage of goods or passengers.

Tachograph

A Tachograph is a mechanical device set in the dash-board of the vehicle, connected to the engine and gear-box, in such a way to accurately record information automatically in graph form on a special circular chart. The EU Regulation covering the use of the Tachograph is EU 3821/85.

Factors recorded are:

(a) vehicle speed
(b) distance travelled
(c) driving time
(d) break periods
(e) work periods
(f) other working time
(g) daily rest periods

The employer *and crew* members shall be responsible for ensuring that the equipment functions correctly and that the seals remain intact. Any operations or interference resulting in falsified readings or recordings is prohibited.

Benefits from Tachograph use:

The Tachograph, called by many a driver "the spy in the cab" has produced a number of benefits: ***

(1) the intended benefit - fewer accidents
(2) guaranteed break and rest periods
(3) more efficient record keeping
(4) improved general administration
(5) less paper-work for the driver
(6) improved route planning
(7) better driving - less engine ware
(8) lower fuel consumption
(9) longer engine life
(10) more accurate planned maintenance

Tested to make sure its working properly

Calibration and Sealing of Tachograph Equipment

To comply with the law, all Tachograph equipment must be calibrated and sealed at an approved workshop. An installation plaque must be affixed to or in the Tachograph head, showing the name, address or trade name of the approved workshop. Inscribed on the plaque must appear the actual measurements relating to the suitable calibration of the Tachograph in the specific vehicle. The date on which these measurements were made, must also appear on the plaque. Under the legislation, absence of an installation plaque is equivalent to not having a correctly installed Tachograph; and renders the vehicle's owner or, where the vehicle is leased, the operator, liable to prosecution.

In the majority of cases in which new vehicles have Tachographs installed as original equipment, no installation plaque is fitted. In such cases the Tachograph equipment must be calibrated and sealed at an approved workshop *before the vehicle is put into service*

The Tachograph must be checked every two years by an authorised Tachograph fitter or workshop. It must also be re-calibrated every six years and a new installation plaque must be fitted.
Note, the inspection carried out under the vehicle roadworthiness test *does not* meet these requirements.

Tachograph - Government Authority

Forbairt (formerly Eolas), Glasnevin, Dublin 9 is the Government authority with responsibility for the approval of workshops to install, calibrate and seal Tachographs. This work can only be carried out at approved workshops. A list of approved workshops is available from the Department of Public Enterprise, Dublin, 2.

It is an offence not to have a Tachograph installed, calibrated and in use in a vehicle to which the Regulations apply and a fine not exceeding IR£1,000 or six months imprisonment or both may be imposed.

***A small number of Irish-International drivers were asked for their opinions on the Tachograph, by the writer, and their views were summarized as follows:**

> **"The Tachograph is OK for the continent, but not for Ireland which is really too small a geographical area".**
> **" There are many breaches of the rules in Ireland".**
> **"'Nine hours a day', that's a laugh; twelve is more like it".**
> **"The number of spot-checks by officers on Irish roads are very few".**
> **" I know other drivers who tell me that the pressure of delivery times imposed by their bosses encourage infringement of the EU regulations".**
> **" Tachograph regulations are strictly enforced in the UK".**
> **"I have recently gone back to driving after a few years, and there seems to be more respect for the Tachograph now".**

19 Road Haulage Licensing - National and International

***National Licence** -*
Requirements for companies operating trucks within the Irish Republic

(1). A Road Freight Carrier's Licence if company carries goods for "Hire or Reward" in vehicles over 2.5 tonnes.

(2). The owner or other employee designated as the Transport Manager, must have a National CPC - (Certificate of Professional Competence*).
(Up to Fiscal year 1999 a National Licence lasts three years and costs IR£55 plus IR£75 per truck).

Exemptions: No Carrier's Licence is required if:

(a) the company is carrying its *own* goods in its *own* vehicles driven by the owner or an employee, or if

(b) the company proposes to carry farm produce or livestock *within the Republic of Ireland only*, as per an approved list of commodities e.g. moving wheat, oats or barley to a place of storage during the Autumn months.

***International Licence** -*
Requirements for companies operating trucks Internationally including journeys to Britain and Northern Ireland.

(1). An International Road Freight Carrier's Licence and EU Community Authorization, if the company is carrying goods for "Hire or Reward" in vehicles over 2.5 tonnes.
(If company is carrying its *own* goods in its *own* vehicles driven by the owner or an employee, a *Carrier's Licence is not required).*

(2). An EU community Authorization and a copy of the Authorization for *each* truck, which come with the International Road Freight Carrier's Licence.

(3). The owner or other employee designated as the Transport Manager, must have an International CPC - (International Certificate of Professional Competence*).
(Up to Fiscal year 1999 a National Licence lasts five years and costs IR£55 plus IR£180 per truck).

The original documents should be kept at the operations base, and a copy of the licence and one of the certified copies of the EU Community Authorization kept in each truck.

*** Courses leadind to examination in Professional Compedence are organized by the Chartered Institute of Transport in Ireland, telephone (01) 676 3188.**

EU Requirements for Obtaining a Carrier's Licence

The applicant must meet the following criteria

1. Be of good repute
2. Satisfy Professional Competence -CPC
3. Be of appropiate financial standing

These EU requirements must be satisied at all times, and failure to do so can lead to the revocation or suspension of a carrier's licence.

An explanation of the required criteria;

1. *Good Repute.*

Applicants must declare if any "relevant"offences have been recorded against them in the previous five-year period. A"relevant" offence is an offence listed on information sheet #RFCL/INFO 5 supplied with the application form, and includes such offences as;

(a) any offence under any Road Traffic Act Red Light.

(b) any offence under the Offences against the State Act

(c) any offence under section 10 or 11 of the International Carriage of Perishable Foodstuffs Act 1987 (#20 of 1987) Drugs/People

2. *Professional Competence.*

There must be one person in the haulage firm, over 18 years of age and of good repute who holds the relevant Certificate of Professional Competence, who can be designated as Transport Manager

3. *Appropiate Financial Standing*

(a) An applicant must not be a bankrupt.

(b) An applicant must be a holder of a current Tax Clearance/C2 Certificate issued by the Revenue Commissioners.

(c) Applicant must have *as a minimum*, the lower of:the following:

3000 EUROs per vehicle over 2.5 tonnes unladen weight

or

150 EUROs per tonne of the maximum authorized weight per vehicle to be authorized for use under the Carrier's Licence

(d) An applicant must have all vehicles proposed for use in Road Freight business in a roadworthy condition. Vehicles must be validly taxed and insured. Every vehicle must have its tachograph calibrated as per EU Regulation 3821/85.

The Transport Manager - Road

A "Transport Manager" is defined as a person who -

(a) holds a Certificate of Competence, and

(b) is of good repute and over 18 years of age, and

(c) is designated in writing, and is engaged to *continually and effectively* manage the transport operations of road freight business.
(In general, *unless the designated Transport Manager is the owner partner, or a director*, persons who have other full-time employment outside the road freight business are not acceptable as transport managers)

All persons employed as Transport Managers should be registered as same with the Revenue Commissioners.

This Section was edited from the Department of Public Enterprise "Guide To Road Haulage Licencing", with permission, and it is not a legal interpretation of the relevant legislation.

20 Transportation of Dangerous Goods

ROAD

ADR Regulations governing the conveyance of Dangerous Substances by road are contained in -

Dangerous Substances (Conveyance of Scheduled Substances by Road (Trade or Business) Regulations 1980 and 1986 (Statutory Instruments Nos. 235 of 1980, and 269 of 1986).

Dangerous Substances (Conveyance of Scheduled Substances by Road (Trade or business) Amendment Regulations 1986 (Statutory Instrument No. 268 of 1986).

EU Council Directive 94/55/EC of 21/11/1994 provides for the approximation of the laws of Member States, and was given effect in the ROI by Statutory Instrument No. 311 0f 1997

RAIL

RID Regulations governing the International Transport of Dangerous Substances by ***Rail*** are contained in EU Regulation number 96-49-EU(EC) 23/7/1996.

SEA

IMDG Regulations governing the International Transport of Dangerous Substances by ***Sea*** are contained in EU Regulation number 93/75/EEC. (Statutory Instrument No 229 of 1995 refers.)

INLAND WATERWAYS

ADN Regulations govern the International Transport of Dangerous Substances by ***Inland Waterways***

AIR TRANSPORT has internationally agreed conventions since 1973.
International Civil Aviation Organization, *ICAO annexe no 18 to Document No.9284 - AN/905 IATA* Regulations govern the International Carriage of Dangerous Goods by ***Air.*** (SI No 224 of 1973 refers)

Statutory Instruments can be bought from the Government Publications Sales Office, Molesworth Street, Dublin 2. A guide to the regulations can be obtained free of charge from the Dept.of Public Enterprise.
Additional information (on Road) for reference purposes only is given in Appendix 1.

The EU 1980 regulations referred to above apply to the twenty-five substances that were declared to be dangerous by the Minister for Labour under the Dangerous Substances Act 1972. These substances are listed hereover. The provisions of the 1980 regulations are, in general, based on the requirements of the European Agreement concerning the International Carriage of Dangerous Goods by Road (ADR). They are enforced by the Industrial Inspectorate of the Department of Public Enterprise in co-operation with the Gárdaí.
The 1986 amending regulations were made by the Minister for Labour on 28th July 1986. They came into operation on 1st January 1987 and on that day they amended the 1980 Regulations. The main purpose of the amendments is to take account of the Dangerous Substances Act 1972 and Amendments to the ADR which were drawn-up by the United National Economic Commission for Europe in 1957.

Substances Declared to be Dangerous under Dangerous Substances Act 1972

The following substances were listed as dangerous under the Dangerous Substances Act 1972 and were contained in Statutory Instrument No. 235 of 1980, 268 of 1986, 269 of 1986, and 311 of 1997.

Acetone	Formic Acid	Potassium Cyanide
Acrylonitrile	Hydrochloric Acid	Potash Lye
Ammonia	Hydrofluoric Acid	Propane
Benzene	Hydrogen Peroxide	Sodium Cyanide
Butane	Methanol Peroxide	Soda Lye
Chlorine	Methyl Acrylate	Sulphuric Acid
Ethanol	Methyl Ethyl	Toluene
Ethyl Acrylate	Ketone	Xylene
	Nitric Acid	

and any substance consisting of a mixture of butane and propane.

Classes of Dangerous Goods as defined in Annexe A to EU Council Directive No. 94/55/EC

(Statutory Instrument No. 311 of 1997 refers)

Class 1	*Explosive substances and articles*
Class 2	*Gases: compressed, liquefied or dissolved under pressure*
Class 3	*Flammable liquids*
Class 4.1	*Flammable solids*
Class 4.2	*Substances liable to spontaneous combustion*
Class 4.3	*Substances which, in contact with water, emit flammable gases*
Class 5.1	*Oxidizing substances*
Class 5.2	*Organic peroxides*
Class 6.1	*Toxic substances*
Class 6.2	*Infectious substances*
Class 7	*Radioactive material*
Class 8	*Corrosive substances*
Class 9	*Miscellaneous dangerous substances and articles*

Conveyance of Dangerous Goods by Road and Rail

Amendment Regulations 1986 - Definitions

Road

A.D.R. *Means the European Agreement concerning the International Carriage of Dangerous Goods by Road.*

Consignor	Is any person who supplies a scheduled substance for conveyance by road in or on a vehicle from a place in the EU. Thus a manufacturer, the occupier of a tank farm, the occupier of a warehouse *or a shipping company* could be a consignor.
Container	Included in this definition is a freight-container.
Packaging	The term *packaging* is not used in a restrictive sense here. It includes conventional packaging as well as tanks, tank containers, demountable tanks, etc.
Scheduled Substance	The definition in the 1980 Regulations has been amended by the 1986 Regulations to include any substance falling within the classes of substances referred to in the schedule to the Dangerous Substances Act 1972. (Part IV Declaration Order 1986). A scheduled substance is a dangerous substance for the purpose of the Dangerous Substances Act 1972.
Vehicle	This is a goods vehicle within the meaning of the Road Traffic (Construction, Equipment and Use of Vehicles) Regulations 1963, an articulated vehicle within the meaning of the said regulations, a semi-trailer within the meaning of the said regulations or a trailer within the meaning of the said regulations.

Rail

R.I.D. *Means the European Agreement concerning the International Transport of Dangerous Goods by Rail*

The EU Regulation number is 96-49-EU 23/7/1996. This Regulation came into affect on the 1st January 1997. Although Iarnród Éireann is unaffected by this legislation for international transportation of dangerous substances; they have decided to carry goods to those standards.

Hazchem Identification

Signs for Vehicles Carrying Dangerous Substances

HAZCHEM IDENTIFICATION

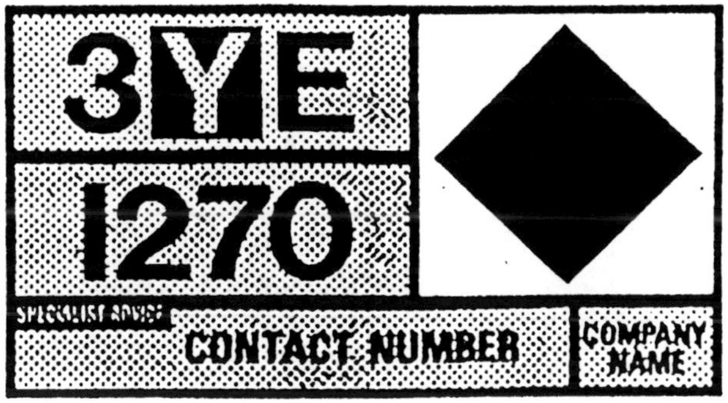

V 156 700 X 400 mm

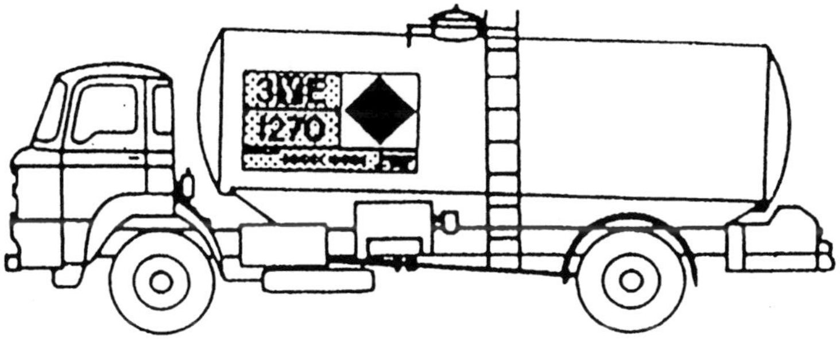

COMPOSITE SIGN FOR THE MARKING OF TANKERS CARRYING DANGEROUS SUBSTANCES CIA AND ADR SPECIFICATIONS.

AVAILABLE IN ALUMINIUM OR SELF-ADHESIVE VINYL.

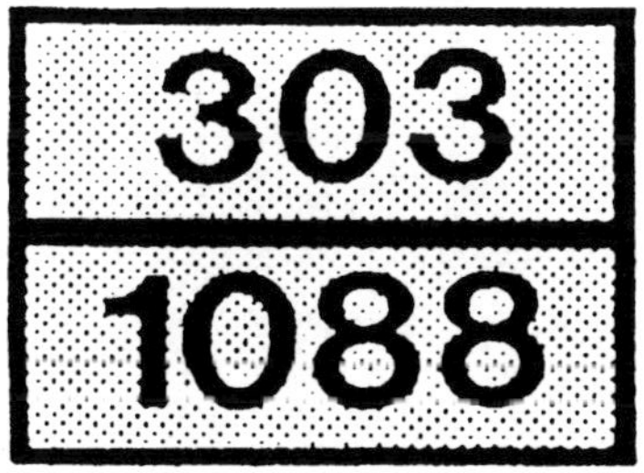

ADR SIGN FOR VEHICLES OTHER THAN TANKERS CARRYING DANGEROUS SUBSTANCES AVAILABLE BOTH REFLECTIVE AND NON REFLECTIVE, ALUMINIUM OR SELF-ADHESIVE VINYL.

FRAMES FOR MOUNTING ALSO AVAILABLE.

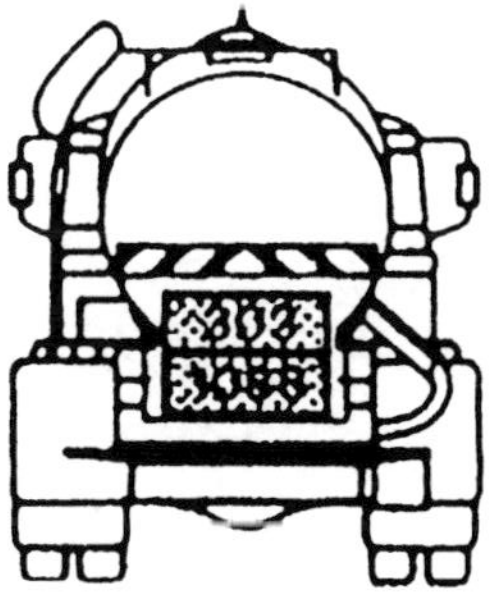

Hazchem Identification Scheme:

With the advances made in technology, the likelihood of companies receiving, stocking, and using Dangerous Chemicals is increased. It follows that companies have a duty, not only to their staff and customers, but also to those living in proximity, to train their staff in the handling of dangerous substances.

The ***Hazchem Code*** is a method of labelling vehicles carrying dangerous cargoes.
The labelling scheme is intended to give the emergency services Gárdaí, Fire Brigade, Ambulances and other persons the information they require to deal with any serious problem involving hazardous substances.

The ***Hazchem*** label is divided into five sections entitled:

1. ***Hazchem Code***
   The members of emergency services carry a reference card containing the Hazchem code numbers of substances being carried.
   The reference card gives basic information regarding the potential danger of the chemicals being carried.

2. ***The UN Number***
   The United Nations code for the chemical, mainly intended for the identification and control of the chemical during loading and unloading.

3. ***Specialist Advice***
   This is an emergency phone number of the manufacturer of the chemical being transported, where specialist advice will be available.

4. ***The Warning Diamond***
   This is an internationally accepted symbol indicating the nature of the hazard.

5. ***The Company Logo***
   The Logo or name of the manufacturer.

21 Water Transportation - Inland Waterways and the Sea

Introduction

Inland Waterways, canals and rivers, at one time were a very important mode of transport to Ireland. Today it is mainly tourists who use this transport mode.

Unlike the canals and rivers of continental Europe which continue to play an important part in the movement of goods, waterways transport in the UK, and especially in Ireland is virtually a memory. The Grand Canal Co. transported goods, mainly stout beer and turf, along the waterways up to the time they were taken over by Córas Iompair Éireann in the 1950s.

Water Transportation's main advantages are smoothness of movement and cheapness. These advantages are outweighed by the main disadvantage - slowness. In the US, inland waterways, one of the earliest modes of American freight movement, are protected by the federal government in a number of ways, including providing low interest capital to vessel operators.

The Importance of Barge Carriers in continental Europe

The first ocean voyage of a barge carrier was reported in 1969. The rationale behind barge carriers is the profitable carriage of goods not really suited to container transport. Public concern over energy problems and environmental pollution appears to favour the increased use of river estuaries and inland waterways for freight movement. Barge containers are waterborne, and being able to load and unload at coastal *and* inland locations, not open to normal shipping, they can allow such traffic to be international without trans-shipment.

In concept, barge carriers could be totally independent of ports, which are liable to congestion.
The main disadvantage, is the requirement for heavy investment in lifting and stowing gear, for ship/barge cargo transfers.

Sea Transport

Introduction

Because of Ireland's geographical location, the facilitation of inland water and sea transport is of paramount importance to its economy. Due to its very high capacity relative to the motive power employed, water transport can offer cheaper transport rates than any alternative form of transport, i.e. economy of scale through capability of moving bulk amounts.

Sea is an important link with overseas markets.

There are five basic classes of ships or seagoing vessels

Liners:

These carry passengers and cargo, operate to fixed time-tables and follow fixed routes. This makes it possible to give firm delivery dates for shipments. As Liner freight costs are high, they are suitable for high value cargoes only.

Cargo Liners:

They operate on fixed routes, often carrying a small number of passengers. They sail to a regular timetable, always leaving port on time, even if all scheduled consignments have not arrived at the docks.

Tramp Ships:

These have neither fixed routes nor fixed timetables. They go where business takes them, and may be chartered for either a specific voyage or a time voyage.

Coastal Shipping:

This is an alternative to inland transport for bulky items. It may be cheaper to send bulky goods round the coast instead of inland. Some large ocean tankers are too big to gain access to some ports or refineries so their cargo may be discharged into coasters in order to complete the journey.

Bulk Carriers:

These vessels are designed for special purposes: e.g. oil tankers and beer tankers. Some refrigerated vessels are also available for transporting perishables over long distances.

Other Types are:

Cellular Container Ships
Ferries - Roll-on/Roll-off
Large Crude Oil Carriers
LNG (Liquefied Natural Gas) Carriers.
Refined Petroleum Products
Automobile Carriers
Tankers - oil and other bulk liquids.

Facilities Required at Ports

In relation to sea transport, the following facilities are required for shipping:

- deep water,
- shelter from rough seas,
- wharves with lifting gear: cranes etc.,
- customs facilities including bonded stores,
- warehouses with specialist storage facilities e.g. for refrigerated food or hazardous cargo. ,
- long, or medium term docking facilities,
- dry-dock facility for repairs,
- ships supplies availability,
- good links with road and rail,
- and around the clock Pilot (guide) availability.

Ship Charters

Shipping is essential to world trade and sea transport is used for a lot of Ireland's imports and exports. Vessels in the shipping trade can be used either by the owner or by charter. The chartering of a ship is made by an agreement called a "Charter Party", of which there are three kinds:

Voyage Charter: The charter has the use of the ship or part of it for a definite voyage or voyages.

Time Charter: The charter has the use of the ship for a specified time.
In both the voyage and time charter the ship is *always* under the control of the ship's owner and all the ship's crew and officers are employees of the shipping company.

Demise Charter: The control of the ship is transferred to the chartered., i.e. firms hiring ships, supply their own crew and officers.

Sea Transport - Advantages and Disadvantages

Advantages

1. It is a suitable way for transporting bulky goods, often over long distances.

2. There are no costs involved in using the seas.

3. Modern ships can carry huge loads of goods.

4. Improved facilities at ports for loading/unloading have speeded up the flow of goods on to, and off the ships.

5. Over long distances it provides a reliable system for carrying goods and people.

6. It is cheaper to send goods by ship than by air. This makes it possible for many companies to market their goods abroad. It is the better choice, when speed is not important.

7. It is flexible in terms of the variety of alternatives available.

8. Many newer ships are designed with sterns that permit FLT loading and unloading.

Disadvantages

1. It is a very slow form of transport.

2. Ships sail to fixed time schedules.

3. On very busy routes it may be difficult to secure a berth for a ship.

4. Fog or very bad weather conditions can cause the cancellation of the journey.

5. Missed tides cause delays.

6. Insurance costs for transporting goods by sea are higher than those for air transport. because the goods are longer in transit.

7. The need to double handle cargo increases the risk of damage to the goods or packaging.

8. Strikes and congestion at ports in the Middle East and in Africa have led to ships queuing for months to be unloaded.

1. Larne 2 Dublin 3 Rosslare 4. Cork

Ferries

Roll-on/Roll-off (RORO) Service

This system consists of the through-transport of goods from a manufacturer's plant, (or from some another distribution point), direct to a customer's premises abroad. Method: goods are loaded onto a vehicle, and then driven *onto* a ship (ferry).

If necessary, the goods can be loaded onto the vehicle in the presence of a customs officer who seals the consignment. The driver travels as a passenger, and at the arrival port can drive the vehicle to its final destination and deliver the goods.

Advantages

1. It is a speedy method of transport, *if ferry schedules are correctly timed into the route plan.*

2. It is cheaper than other forms of transport, especially for complete unit loads with single origin and destination points.

3. The owner is in possession of the goods at all times.

4. It can be arranged for the return journey to collect and bring back a suitable consignment.

5. Frequent sailings, coupled with flexible road transport scheduling , provide regular scheduled services.

6. EDI technology is gradually reducing delays caused by paper-work systems not keeping up with the speed of the RORO system itself.

Disadvantages

1. There may be delays on the return journey.

2. Extra insurance costs will be incurred for taking the lorry abroad.

3. Roll-on/ Roll-off advantage is lost when used for less than lorry sized loads. Groupage systems will need to be used ,causing double-handling, and extra packaging.

22 The Channel Tunnel

The Birth of EuroTunnel

During the 1980's, the UK and French Governments held an open competition, to design a practical means of sending people and freight between England and France; other than by air or sea. The purpose of the competition was to find a way to improve transit times and reliability of freight movements between the UK and continental Europe.
There were some innovative designs including various types of bridges to span the stretch of sea between the two countries. In the end, the competion was won by TML for their design; *a tunnel under the bed of the sea.* TML a consortium set-up for the competion, was composed of construction companies, five from the UK and five from France. TML having won the competition, were in the unusual situation of having to *invent*, as it turned out, a company to use the tunnel. EuroTunnel was born, *financed completely from private sources.*

EuroTunnel - the Owners

Many of the worlds' banks are the investors, approximately 80%, with the balance financed from public-buying on the Paris (in the main) and London stock exchanges. Partly due to a one year delay in opening, the EuroTunnel operators faced debts totalling billions of pounds. By September 1998, the situation had greatly improved, because some banks had exchanged debts for equity.

The Service

Transportation of Train Passengers, Reformed Trainloads of freight and RORO freight on the Shuttle service are provided for, by EuroTunnel. The fast travelling time of this rail link system of 35 minutes is usually unaffected by the type of bad weather that delays ferry-crossings.
Freight is reformed into viably sized trainloads at Doncaster, Bescot and Wembly This would include feeder.traffic from Ireland. In Bescot (near Birmingham) and Wembly, freight trainloads are sorted and put onto separate trains bound for various destinations in mainland Europe after arrival at Calais. Some trains of freight travel via the tunnel to Lille in France, where the sorting takes place.

Ireland and the Channel Tunnel.

Since the opening of the Channel Tunnel in 1994, the Republic of Ireland is *the only member state of the EU cut-off from mainland Europe.*
The lorry shuttle service between Folkestone and Calais is not likely to prove much quicker for Irish (Republic.) freight currently using RORO methods. This is due to the *over transit time* from Ireland to EU cities.
Currently RORO traffic to and from continental Europe uses the routes detailed below.

(a) sailing from Irish port direct to European port(s),
(b) sailing from Irish ports, and driving through the UK,
(c) sailing from ports in NI, and driving through the UK.

The question ***still*** *to be answered, is*:

"Will the Channel Tunnel alter the traditional pattern of Irish RORO traffic"?

Advantages and Disadvantages of the Channel Tunnel in the context of Irish driver use.

Advantages

1. When there is a satisfactory solution to its huge financial problems, and when freight-volumes reach the carrying capacity originally envisaged, the Channel Tunnel operation could lead to a reduction in the overall freight cost of shipments. This could happen in one of two ways:

(a) *Speed*

The shorter crossing time allows for some driving on arrival in France.
The faster travel time, obviously reduces travel-time costs,

(b) *Competition with Traditional Ferry Traffic*

Already P&O and Stena lines have worked together on a partial merger, to consolidate their position. Their charges have reduced.
An Irish media report in 1996* indicated that Irish companies would also look at joint ventures, to improve costs and service frequency to customers.
[One such company was Bell Lines. Unfortunately storm damage to key dock equipment, and other problems caused that company to cease trading. Since then, there has been little comment on Irish companies merging or setting-up joint ventures.]

2. Dock facilities at Calais are excellent. Freight for most of the Continent can pass through Calais.

Disadvantages

1. Even if the operation leads directly or indirectly to the lowering of road haulage vehicle rates to continental Europe via the Tunnel or by RORO ferry; the Irish Sea crossing still has to be made, followed by *a journey on the congested UK road network.*
2. Of its nature, being a long tunnel, a major tragedy could result from a "minor" accident, or small fire.
3. In time, safety concerns, are likely to restrict the transportation of combustible materials, *and* products containing a small percentage of those hazardous ingredients.

The Future

The 35 45 minute trip through the Channel Tunnel only counts towards a driving *Break* under EU Regulations (EU 3820/85) on driving hours; whereas a ferry crossing can count towards a *Rest* period. A longer ferry crossing, for example Rosslare to Le Harve used as a *Rest* period, may well be of greater benefit to many Irish drivers. *However the "Irish Ferries" line reports a sizeable increase in the numbers of Irish RORO vehicles using the Eurotunnel in the 12 months ending August 1998.*
If improved rail-freight links are developed in the UK to and from ports on the western coast, (e.g. Holyhead), a result could well be an increase in traffic-flow between Ireland and the Continent, using *unaccompanied RORO* traffic on trailers or using containers on a LOLO (Lift-on/Lift-off) mode.

* (**"The Sunday Business Post" Page 4 8th September 1996**)

23 Rail Transport

Introduction

Rail was the main mode of inland transport up to the early 1900s. As the decades went by, the importance of rail transport in the lives of the population was reduced by an improving standard of living enabling many to procure their own means of transport. The pony and trap, the bicycle and the increasing flexibility of road transport made rail transport less attractive for shorter journeys. Most European nations experienced this change.

Rail transport is best suited to carrying bulk loads over long distances. Many refrigerated products are sent by rail in other countries but, because of the size of Ireland, distances to be covered are relatively short. Road transport gains the "edge" over rail because of this, and also because it is a more flexible mode of transport.

Types of Rail Transport available

In the Republic of Ireland the national rail network is run by Iarnród Éireann, (part of C.I.É).
In Northern Ireland, the rail network it is run by N.I.R. (Northern Ireland Rail).
Services offered by Iarnród Éireann include the following:

1. Bulk Transport

2. Container Rail

3. Fastrack
   Same-day service to over 80 cities and towns. Fastrack can also fly parcels to the UK and deliver them to their destinations by the UK InterCity 'Red-Star'service. A fast service to Belfast with delivery to the customer is also offered.

4. Passenger Transport. Iarnród Éireann provide three passenger transport services:

Inter City	A service connecting provincial cities and towns throughout Ireland.
DART	A suburban commuter service set up by the government to provide a fast and efficient rail system for the large population living between Howth on the north side of Dublin and Bray(Greystones by 1999) in County Wicklow. This is an electrically powered network as opposed to the rest of the country's rail system which is diesel powered. For outlying areas not directly located on the Howth to Bray line a DART bus feeder service is provided. (DART: Dublin Area Rapid Transport system).
ARROW	A suburban commuter service set up by the government to provide an additional facility, serving north-west Dublin and Kildare stations.

Types of Rail Transport available (continued)

LUAS

The proposed LRT - Light Rail Transit system , funded by the EU, will be set up by CIÉ at the request of the Oireachtas.

This will be a system using European made electric Tram-Cars holding 200 passengers, *most of whom will be standing.*
Initially, the LUAS will serve the Dublin areas of Sandyford, Dundrum, Tallaght, and later Ballymun and Dublin Airport.
Construction was originally planned to start by March 1997 at the latest. This did not take place.
The 1997 newly elected government called for yet another feasibility study. Construction of a short subway section, through the city centre is under consideration.

Current Situation
In July 1998 revised completion dates were issued as follows:
Winter 2002 for Tallaght to O'Connell street to Connolly Station,
Spring 2003 for Sandyford to St Stephen's green.
No date yet for Broadstone to Ballymun to Dublin Airport.
No date yet for Subway from St Stephen's Green to Broadstone, although this was discussed again in the Dáil in October 1999.
For future consideration are branch lines which will link Clondalkin, Cabinteely, Finglas, Swords, and the Docklands, to the main network.

Great inconvenience and disruption of traffic for some years will result from the digging up of roads and the relocation of water, gas, electricity, and telecommunications facilities.

This would not be the case if a Trolley-Car system were chosen for the LUAS. Apparently this has never been considered?

The LUAS
The purpose is to provide a frequent service for people, which will:

(a) reduce the number of private cars congesting the city traffic; and

(b) reduce pollution of the atmosphere.

Rail Transport - Advantages and Disadvantages

Advantages

1. All railways service the main parts of their countries, and this is of vital importance for industrialists who import or export materials.
2. Differential rates are charged, the larger the quantity moved the lower the unit cost.
3. Rail offers the facility of speed over long distances and is much faster than Road transport.
4. Large consignments of goods can be handled very easily.
5. Trains are less liable to delay by bad weather.
6. Containers can be transported by rail. In most countries this is done at night when the lines are free of other traffic.
7. Rail reduces the hazards to the environment resulting from road vehicle exhaust fumes.

Diesel Intercity Train in [illegible]

Disadvantages

1. There is a lot of handling of the goods; this is potentially dangerous, especially in the case of fragile items.
2. A long distance between the factory or other distribution point, and the railway station, may be very inconvenient.
3. Trains operate only at specified times.
4. Not every town is serviced by rail so the train will only bring the goods to the nearest town.
5. It is expensive for short journeys and also for small loads.
6. Many companies have closed down their railway sidings, e.g. Guinness
7. Shunting shocks may cause damage, to goods.

24 Air Transport

Introduction

Air space is a natural resource and no investment in it is required. Air transport can be used to transport goods within a country, or between countries separated by large mountain ranges, or by large expanses of water. This immediately gives it certain advantages over Road and Rail transport.

Air Transport in Ireland

In the early 1930s commercial flights of freight and passengers started. The inaugural commercial flight of the National Airline - Aer Lingus, was in April 1936, from Dublin to Bristol. By the end of Aer Lingus's first year in business, the total weight of cargo (mainly newspapers and mail), was about 3 tonnes. In 1947 their total cargo weight was 394 tonnes.
Fifty years later in 1997 the cargo figure was 34,759 tonnes - a huge increase.

At the begininng of 1998, the US aircraft company, Boeing, estimated the world-wide airfreight market to grow at a percentage of 6-7% *year on year* to 2015. This rate, *as a minimum*, will apply to Ireland.

Airfreight Cargo Figures

Aer Lingus	*1936-37*	*1947*	*1997*	*1998*	*1999*
				(including mail)	*(including mail)*
Tonnes Carried	3	394	34759	45000	47000 (estimate.)

Air cargo - Passenger and Airfreight-only Operators

Passenger

Today, 80% of air freight the world over is carried on *passenger* aircraft. The thinking behind this is quite straight forward. Cargo freight will subsidize undersold passenger seats, or large passenger numbers will subsidize under capacity freight sales.

Airfreight-only Operators and Integrators

There are of course successful *airfreight-only operators*, mainly of US origin.
Up to the early 1980s the typical method used for *air express cargo* was a system in which the freight forwarder collected and consolidated parcels, delivered them to a chosen airline, having arranged preparation of custom clearance entries for the cargo at the destination airport. The cargo would then be collected by an associate company of the forwarder, for delivery to the customer.
With this type of system all the activities in the supply chain were *segregated* - delays were common.
Recognising the logic of *integrating* these activities, Fred Smith of Federal Express is credited with being the first to introduce, what is often now called the "*Integrator*" carrier concept.* By buying their own aircraft and road vehicles, the customer's parcel was in the care of the carrier, from collection to delivery. Integrators like DHL, FedEx, TNT, and UPS show growth rates in 1995, 1996, 1997 and 1998 of over 10% year on year.

* **After/From "logisticssolutions" magazine of NITL August 1998**

Air Freight Costs

Air cargo has an undisputed advantage over other modes of transport in four basic transport "quality criteria", *Speed, Reliability, Frequency, and the Environment for carriage.*

The cost of air transport is high, but this must be weighed against total savings *including time*. The reduction in pilferage, and savings on packaging materials, are but two examples.

The Air transport industry has seen major developments since the Second World War. Military Logistics systems and other technologies devised out of necessity in wartime, were later made available to cost-conscious commercial aircraft companies in subsequent years. There have been important developments in the areas of integrated unit loads. The rapid growth in this mode of transport is likely to continue. Development still continues.

The Airline freight rates charged and the regulations governing air transport are detailed in a book entitled *"The Air Cargo Tariff"*. This is used by all users of Air transport.

Rates are generally expressed as a price for a weight unit, (kg).

Three basic types of rates are known as:

"General Cargo Rates" (GC) and

Specific Commodity Rates" (SC).

In addition, special Unitised Load Device (ULD) rates, Container rates, and Classified rates are also published.

Specific Commodity Rates

These rates offer a substantial reduction in costs compared with the general rates. A shipper may try to have a specific commodity rate established for air transport between specific airports if he ships a large quantity of a specific type of cargo. Application may be made to an airline which then submits it, together with its own recommendation, to I.A.T.A. After all member airlines have been consulted the rate is either accepted and published, or rejected.

Consolidation Rates

Special consolidation (air 'groupage') rates are available from any forwarder.

No need to know

Methods of Air-Cargo Transportation

Since the National Airline's purchase of 321 and 330 Air Buses, the method of carrying freight has changed. Containers called Igloos which fit the contours of the superstructure of Boeing 707s, and 737s account for only 5% of freight shipped. The method, growing in use since 1995, is the use of airline pallets of different capacity-sizes which are rolled into the aircraft along floor rails. This saves a lot of time compared to older materials handling methods.

The pallets are constructed from aluminium and light steel. Cargo received from shipping companies must arrive 90 minutes before aircraft take-off, to allow time for loading onto the special pallets.For long haul journeys, goods are received from Cargo Agents, the night before the day-time flight, and are loaded onto airline pallets.

ULD *(IATA name)*	**TYPE**	**AIRCRAFT**	**VOLUME**
RAK	LD7	A330	10 cubic meters *(350 cubic feet)*
TARE WEIGHT 404 kgs.		MAX. GROSS WEIGHT 4629 kgs.	
INTERNAL DIMENSIONS Base Length 307 cms *(121 inches)*	INTERNAL DIMENSIONS Width 214 cms *(84 inches)*	INTERNAL DIMENSIONS Height 157 cms *(62 inches)*	
ULD *(IATA name)*	**TYPE**	**AIRCRAFT**	**VOLUME**
AKH	---	A321	3.4 cubic meters *(120 cubic feet)*
TARE WEIGHT 76 kgs.		MAX. GROSS WEIGHT 1134 kgs.	
INTERNAL DIMENSIONS Base Length 145 cms *(56.5 inches)*	INTERNAL DIMENSIONS Width 141 cms *(55.5 inches)*	INTERNAL DIMENSIONS Height 109 cms *(43 inches)*	
ULD *(IATA name)*	**TYPE**	**AIRCRAFT**	**VOLUME**
PMC	---	A330	12.7 cubic meters *(450 cubic feet)*
TARE WEIGHT 140 kgs.		MAX. GROSS WEIGHT 5103 kgs.	
INTERNAL DIMENSIONS Base Length 307 cms *(121 inches)*	INTERNAL DIMENSIONS Width 232 cms *(92 inches)*	INTERNAL DIMENSIONS Height 157cms *(62 inches)*	

Air Transport - Advantages and Disadvantages

Advantages

1. It is the speediest form of transport available and this obviously reduces delivery times.
2. "Lead-time" advantage. Because of the speed of airfreight, local stocks of materials need not be carried in every country; thereby reducing the "cost of storage", e.g. many Ford and Fiat car parts are supplied to most European countries from central depots in the UK.
3. Air freight reduces the risk of damage by pilferage.
4. It is most suitable for the transportation of perishable goods.
5. Expert and speedy customs clearance facilities are available at airports.
6. Less packaging is required; if ground handling is not too rough.
7. Helicopters can be used successfully where fixed-wing aircraft cannot gain access; e.g. mountainous regions, off-shore oil rigs, and certain military operations.
8. Ideal for transporting delicate equipment which requires smooth transit.

Disadvantages

1. It is a very costly method of transport, especially in comparison with Road and Rail costs.
2. Aircraft may be delayed at airports because of weather conditions.
3. Although airfreight from point to point is very quick, airport congestion can cause delays.
4. There is a limit to the amount of heavy equipment a plane can carry.
5. It is necessary to transport the goods from the factory to the airport and this increases the transport costs, especially if the factory is a long distance from the airport.
6. Flights are normally at fixed times and this may not always suit.

Future Development of Air Freight

Developments in Air Freight are expected to be in the following direction:

1. Larger "Pure Freight" aircraft is the trend in the US, but not to any great extent in Europe. Development of high-capacity jet-freighters may permit lower US transport rates in future.
2. Speedier handling of freight through terminals by using "paperless" EDI systems and electronic tracking. Ratification of the Montreal Protocol No. 4 in June 1998 facilitates this.
3. Greater use of *airline-pallet* loads, speeds up airport loading and unloading.
4. Direct door-to-door container services, relying on the flexibility of road transport.
5. The use of computers for sorting cargo and assembling unit loads.
6. Simplification of international customs procedures, similar to the EU Harmonisation System.
7. Reduction in freight charges.
8. Integrators (express couriers), will handle larger consignments, and become specialists.

The cost of freight handling increases with the number of handling operations. To take advantage of lower freight costs it is necessary to group freight into larger Unit Loads at the earliest possible point in the handling operation.

25 Pipeline

Introduction

Not immediately thought of as being a mode of transport, Pipelines are in fact, a very important rôle player in the movement of essential materials. Domestic water supply, and Kinsale natural gas are but two of the products which are transported by pipeline. In industry they are used for the movement of many chemical liquids from storage tanks to place of manufacture. In the UK and USA this form of transport has long existed.

Crude oil is pumped through pipeline over vast areas of desert in the Middle East.

The Siberian Pipeline scheme was long regarded as one of the world's largest civil construction projects; with many pumping stations across central Russia.

Pipelines are currently being used to move cereals. They are used in mines to move coal and certain ores. The ore is mixed with water and pumped short distances to the surface.

Pipelines - Advantages and Disadvantages

Advantages

1. Once built they cost very little to use.
2. Ongoing maintenance costs are not high.
3. Pipelines, not being affected by the weather, or industrial problems, guarantee an ongoing supply.
4. In comparison to heavy vehicle transport, there are no pollution problems in use.
5. They can operate 24 hrs. a day, 7 days a week , resulting in the movement of vast quantities of material.

Disadvantages

1. They are very costly to build.
2. Limitation of use - pipelines tend to be product specific, used for one purpose only.

26 International Movement of Goods

Introduction
International trade is the buying and selling of materials and services among different countries of the world. Because countries have different climates and different natural resources, it means that they must trade with each other in order to obtain materials which they cannot produce, or find uneconomic to produce.
Dispatching goods from one country to another means complying with the export regulations of one country and the import regulations of another. These regulations vary according to the product and the countries in question. Certain basic documents must be presented at customs; health & safety labelling requirements must be met, and relevant duties and taxes must be paid.

It is important to establish at an early stage, what particular regulations apply. An Bórd Trachtála [The Trade(Export) Board] can help the exporter with relevant information. The board's trade information section publishes the "Irish Exporters' Guide" which sets out country by country the specific import procedures and documentary requirements of all the trading countries of the world. Information on documentation and procedures for importers is provided by the Customs and Excise Service.

The Rôle of the Professional Freight Forwarder

The rôle of the Freight Forwarder in arranging both Exports and Imports continues to be important.
It is universally accepted that Freight Forwarding is an international industry, with its effectiveness depending on the professional competence and skill of forwarders providing service, both at the point of origin and the point of destination. The removal of customs barriers in the EU since 1993, has not diminished this role.

The International Forwarders:

(a) have a large network of contacts world wide, enabling them to offer an integrated service from door to door throughout the world,
(b) freight forwarders offer a wide range of services, including advising customers on the quickest and most economical means of transportation,
(c) forwarders have been pioneers in developing the use of new transport routes. From their experience, they are able to offer customers the kind of routing which is most favourable to the type of goods being shipped,
(d) give expert assessment to any special considerations, such as Bill of Lading requirements, consular document requirements, insurance cover or conditions contained in letters of credit,

Transport costs often determine whether or not products will be competitive on world markets. The forwarder is in a position to draw up full costings for transport and other relevant charges, e.g. customs duties.

International Forwarders provide Advice
In many instances the forwarder plays a vital role in opening up new export markets, and will arrange not only the transportation, but also the distribution of the goods within the country of destination. Packaging plays an important part in transport. "Over-packaged" goods add to both the materials cost and to the weight factor, while "under-packaged" goods are liable to damage. The package shape can also be significant if optimum use is to be made of containers. Forwarders can give invaluable advice in this area and, in particular, with fragile, perishable and dangerous goods.
International Forwarders have Specialist Knowledge of the customs and import licence requirements of the countries to which his customers are exporting. These requirements can vary enormously, from country to country. Some countries have a very relaxed customs regime designed to control, without impeding trade. In other countries, such as Japan, the overriding factor is attention to detail. Paper-work mistakes; a minor omission, an error in calculation or description, gives the Japanese importer a great degree of trouble.
Forwarders will arrange for the completion of the necessary documents. Members of the Institute of Freight Forwarders of Ireland are authorised to use the F.I.A.T.A. combined Transport Bill of Lading. This document is approved by the International Chamber of Commerce and has an excellent reputation and is recognised as one of tradition and trust.
Probably one of the most frustrating parts of a forwarder's job is dealing with import customs documentation. Delays in clearing goods obviously add to the cost which in turn is passed on to the eventual purchaser. Consolidation of goods has always been the prerogative of the forwarder. Whether by surface or air, this means that the forwarder takes many smaller lots which of themselves are inadequate for a full load and brings them together into one load, called a "Unit", and this activity represents a large part of a forwarder's work. The attitudes of shipping lines both here and in the UK differ greatly from that found on the continent. There the Lines recognise the forwarder's role and influence in traffic routing, and actually seek the forwarder's support.
The Relationship that exists between Forwarders and Airlines is much closer than that which exists between forwarders and shipping lines. Traditionally the Irish exporter deals with the Shipping Lines, particularly where full container loads are concerned. This is an understandable concern for big companies, but it is a standing overhead, which must be financed irrespective of the volume of work handled by the shipping department. It is interesting to note that multinationals who have established in Ireland, tend to deal with forwarders. They also take the view that the forwarder has a much wider experience of available services. Compared to setting-up and maintaining their own shipping department, with its overhead costs, they only have to pay the forwarder when his services are used.
The Professional Forwarder has a specific function in the overall handling of the nation's foreign trade. His independent approach to transport matters, allied to his experience of the complexities of overseas shipping, can make a positive contribution to the continued development of Irish export trade.
Groupage:
This is a system of consolidation used to obtain the benefit of cheaper rates for full loads. A Groupage Agent, usually a Freight Forwarding Agent, groups together small consignments from a number of exporters to make up a full container load or vehicle load, covering the complete consignment with a "House Bill of Lading" or some similar document.
At the destination, the consignment is "broken down" into its constituent parts for individual delivery.

Personal Use or Exhibition Carnew no duties or Taxes

Services Offered by the Professional Freight Forwarder

1. Groupage Traffic: The forwarder's particular contribution to the economy.
2. Advice to customers on the quickest and most economical means of transport.
3. Advice to customers on packaging,containers, and outer packing.
4. Customs clearance.
5. Compliance with foreign trade regulations and letter of credit instruction.
6. Choice of the most suitable carrier and the conclusion of the contract of carriage.
7. Insurance coverage during transit.
8. Advice to customers on warehousing and distribution.
9. Provision of Carriers' and forwarders' documents.
10. Supervision of the movement of goods.

Cabotage - Introduction

Cabotage is a freighting term used to describe the movement of cargo from one part of a State to another part of the same State. The word is derived from the French, describing a small boat or coaster contracted to transport merchandise, e.g. wine, from port to port along the coastline.

After seeming disuse for many years, the word was resurrected in the US and apparently became the "property" of the Air-freighting Industry.

Cabotage - The Irish Situation

In the Irish context, since 1st January 1993, Cabotage is the term generally used to describe:- *"point-to-point haulage operations within the territory of one EU Member State by a haulier based in another Member State, i.e. a non-resident operator". This was extended in 1994 to include Norway, Sweden, Suome (Finland), and Iceland.*

A Limited form of Cabotage was introduced in July 1990. *Following agreement in 1993, full road freight Cabotage was introduced throughout the EU on 1st July 1998.*

Advocates of Cabotage say:

(1) Cabotage will reduce the number of wasteful unladen journeys.

(2) It will save on fuel, labour costs, ease traffic congestion, and increase productivity.

(3) To quote the CITI, " an Irish haulier could carry a consignment to Lyon and before picking up a return load for Ireland in Paris, could carry a domestic consignment from Lyon to Paris".

Up to 1997, opponents of Cabotage said:

(1) There is already over capacity in domestic markets.

(2) Ruinous competition from non-resident hauliers will result from their prices being based on marginal costing.

(3) Likely competition from Northern Ireland and mainland UK hauliers in the Irish domestic haulage market. These hauliers have some cost advantages over those based at home.

The Current Situation:

As at August 1998, spokesmen from the road haulage industry say that the reality of the situation presents no threat to the industry, and is not likely to do so in the immediate future.

Mainland EU hauliers are unlikely to compete in the Irish market because:-

(1) there are greater opportunities in the larger mainland market

(2) the need to organize ferry bookings

(3) the dispersed nature of the Irish market

27 Transport Documents

When goods are sent by sea or air, a document is issued by the carrying company. This document serves as a receipt for the goods, and as a contract between the carrier and the shipper. This is a Consignment Note.

The Documents most commonly used are:

1. *The Consignment Note* is both a receipt for goods that have been delivered to a forwarder for transport to a named destination and is evidence of a contract of shipment. It sets out the conditions under which goods are carried. It is NOT A DOCUMENT OF TITLE, which means that the original document does not have to be handed over by the consignee to obtain delivery of the goods. It should set out the details of the consignor, consignee and the goods.

2. *The Bill of Lading* is one of the most important documents in international trade. It is signed by the captain, agents or owners of the vessel, finalising written evidence for the conveyance and delivery of merchandise sent by sea to a named destination.

   A Bill of Lading is important for three reasons:

   (a) It is a receipt for the goods shipped, and provides certain details as to quantity and condition when placed on board the vessel.

   (b) It is evidence of a contract of shipment.

   (c) It is a ***Document of Title*** without which delivery of the goods cannot take place.

   All three points are important to the exporters, but from a practical viewpoint (c) above, which relates to the way in which ***the Bill of Lading conveys ownership in the goods***, is probably the most important as this will have an important bearing on the way the documentary process is linked to the method of payment.

   Types of Bill of Lading (Ocean)

   (a) Clean:

   A term used of a Bill of Lading when the transportation company has not noted irregularities in packing or general condition of all or any part of a shipment.

   (b) Straight:

   A Bill of Lading drawn directly to the consignee and therefore not negotiable.

   (c) Order:

   A bill of Lading drawn to the order of some party, usually the shipper or the bank whose endorsement is required to effect negotiability.The TITLE thereafter passes to the holder.

   (d) Order: "NOTIFY"

   A bill of Lading drawn usually to the order of the shipper or the bank with the additional clause that the consignee is to be notified upon the arrival of the merchandise. However, such mention of the consignee's name does not give him title to the merchandise.

   (e) Through: Bill of Lading

   A Bill of Lading is used when transportation involves two or more carriers.

The Documents most commonly used are (continued)

3. *The Airwaybill, AWB,* is approximately equal to the Seafreight Bill of Lading. It is a form of consignment note used when goods are shipped by air. It also functions as a receipt and is evidence of a CONTRACT OF CARRIAGE. However, the essential difference is that ***it is not a negotiable title to the goods*** in the same way as the shipping Bill of Lading. It is widely used as a valuable receipt and as evidence of dispatch. It can, at times, be used within the framework of payment methods.

Import and Export Documentation

Note: since the 1st of January 1993, exports to other EU member states are called "despatches"; and imports from other EU member states are referred to as "acquisitions". *For ease of writing and understanding, the original words are being used in the following sections of text*

Single Administrative Document (SAD): Not used anymore within EU

Background: The European Union, in its efforts to develop its internal market, took various measures to reduce barriers to trade between Member States. As part of that process it adopted regulations to introduce a harmonised customs declaration form for intra-Community trade in 1988.
This form is known as the Single Administrative Document (SAD).

Advent of the Single Market: Since 1st January 1993 it is no longer necessary for goods traded within the EU to be presented to customs or for the Single Administration Document (SAD) to be completed. However, completion of the Single Administration Document is required for goods traded (imports and exports) with non-EU. countries and these goods will still require customs clearance..

The Form:

1. The SAD form sets are available in two versions, an 8-page version which can be used for export, transit and import formalities and a 4-page dual purpose version which can be used for either export or import formalities.
2. As the principal form sets cater for one item only, continuation form sets (8-page or 4-page, as appropriate) are available for subsequent items.
3. The SAD forms are subject to a charge.
4. Forms must not be filled-in by hand. Word processing and EDI packages are available. All copies of the document must be legible. All relevant boxes must be completed. Each item of data must be contained within its appropriate box or within its appropriate division of a box. To achieve this the typing indicator in Box 2 (the rectangle in the top left hand corner) should be used for the purpose of alignment. Forms must contain no erasures or overwriting. Any alterations must be made by crossing out the incorrect particulars and, where appropriate, adding those required. Any alteration made in this way must be initialled by the person making them and expressly authenticated by customs.

N.B. Forms that are illegible or incomplete, or contain inaccurate information, will be rejected by customs.

Import and Export Documentation (continued)

In order to deter abuse of the VAT system and to ensure that statistics of internal EU trade continues to be collected, two further documents are required:-

The VAT Information Exchange System (VIES) is designed to prevent and deter the abuse of the VAT zero-rating provisions for goods traded in the EU; which charge rate is necessary because VAT rates within the EU are not yet harmonized. An integral part of the VIES arrangement is that each member state must store and process information which it will collect from its exporters about the general level of trade with other member states. Returns for VIES relate only to exports to other EU member states and will be required from all exporters regardless of the annual value of their trade.

The VIES Form returned by businesses to the VIMA Office (Revenue Commissioners), at the end of the required period (three months), is a statement (declaration) of the value of exports and imports shipped to named companies at Zero Rate of VAT from within member states. Information from these forms is entered into an EU EDI computer network so that importers will be charged VAT at the relevant rate for their member state.

Intrastat is designed to ensure that the statistics of internal EU trade continue to be collected. Returns under Intrastat will concern imports from, as well as exports to, other Member States.

Summary of VIES and Intrastat Requirements

Category of Trader	VIES	Intrastat
Exporters to EU Member States	*Complete VIES return quarterly or monthly, annually in limited cases.*	*Complete EU Exports box on VAT 3 form. Plus, if value of exports exceeds £500,000 per annum, also complete detailed INTRASTAT monthly return.*
Importers from EU Member States	*VIES applies only to exports.*	*Complete EU Exports box on VAT 3 form. Plus, if value of imports exceeds £100,000 per annum, also complete detailed Intrastat monthly return.*

28 Incoterms - Buyer's responsibility and Seller's responsibility

"Incoterms" are a set of abbreviations used in international trade whose meanings have been internationally agreed. These are voluntarily used so that both Buyer and Seller will know and understand the terms of delivery under which an item has been bought. These were first published by the International Chamber of Commerce in 1936. These original Incoterms referred to the carriage of materials by ship. They have been continually revised to take account of other modes of transport. Since 1990 and 1992, half the terms cover freight by modes other than sea.

Incoterms and their meanings:

Incoterm	***Meaning***	***Buyer's Responsibility***	***Seller's Responsibility***
EXW	***Ex Works (of Supplier)***	***cost, freight, and risk***	
FCA	***Free Carrier At (a named place)***	***main carriage costs, and risk***	***clears materials for export***
FAS	***Free Alongside (ship, on docks)***	***main carriage costs, and risk, clears materials for export***	
FOB*	***Free on Board (ship)***	***main carriage costs, and risk***	***clears materials for export***
CFR	***Cost and Freight***	***risks during main carriage, plus local carriage costs***	***main carriage costs, plus all costs to destination country, clears materials for export***
CIF	***Cost, Insurance, and Freight***	***risks during main carriage (excluding insurance), plus local carriage costs***	***main carriage and insurance costs, plus all costs to destination country***
CPT	***Carriage Paid To (named place)***	***risks during main carriage, plus local carriage costs***	***main carriage costs, plus all costs to destination country, clears materials for export***
CIP	***Carriage and Insurance Paid To (named destination)***		***main carriage and insurance costs, plus all costs to destination country***
DAF	***Delivered at Frontier (country border)***		***all costs and risks to named destination,clears materials for export***
DES	***Delivered Ex Ship (at specified port)***	***clears materials for import***	***all costs and risks to named destination***
DEQ	***Delivered Ex Quay (at named port of destination)***		***all costs and risks to named destination,duty paid or unpaid as per agreement***
DDU	***Delivered Duty Unpaid (at specified place of destination)***	***clears materials for import, and pays duty***	***all costs and risks to named destination***
DDP	***Delivered Duty Paid (at specified place of destination)***		***all costs and risks to named destination, clears materials for import, including paying duty***

**** To explain it detail one of the frequently used Incoterms - FOB***

FOB means "Free on Board". The materials are placed on board the ship by the sellar at the port of shipment named in the sales contract. The risk of damage or loss to the goods is transferred from the seller to the buyer when the goods pass the ship's rail.

In addition the seller must (a) obtain an export licence, if so required, (b) provide the "customary" packing (packing recognized as the norm and correct for the purpose), (c) pay costs of checking operations, e.g. weighting and counting.

The buyer must (1) reserve space on board a vessel, (2) bear all costs after goods have passed the ship's rail, (3) pay any additional costs should the ship be late or unable to take the goods on board.

Free Domicile Direct to retailer eg Levi's

CFR
Cost and Freight, to a named overseas port of import. Under this term, the seller quotes a price for the goods that includes the cost of transportation to the named point of debarkation. The cost of insurance is left to the buyer's account. (Typically used for ocean shipments only.)Seller owns goods until they are loaded on vessel.

CIF
Cost, Insurance and Freight - to a named overseas port of import. Under this term, the seller quotes a price for the goods (including insurance), all transportation, and miscellaneous charges to the point of debarkation from the vessel. (Typically used for ocean shipments only.)

CPT
Carriage Paid To - Pricing terms indicating that carriage, or carriage and insurance, are paid to the named place of destination. They apply in place of CFR and CIF, respectively, for shipment by every modes ~~other than water~~ -and-

CIP
Carriage and Insurance Paid to a named place of destination. Used in place of CFR and CIF, respectively, for shipment by modes other than water.

CAF
Currency Adjustment Factor is a percentage of ocean freight applied to a shipment to compensate for foreign currency fluctuations.

DAF
Delivered at Frontier, at a named place. -- The seller fulfills his obligation when the goods have been made available, cleared for export, at the named point at the frontier, but before the customs border of the adjoining country. Primarily intended for rail and road transport.

DES
Delivered Ex Ship, at a named port -- the seller fulfills his obligation when the goods have been made available to the buyer on board the ship un-cleared for import at the named port of destination. The seller has to bear all the costs and risks involved in bringing the goods to the named port of destination. Only used for sea or inland waterway transport.

DEQ
Delivered Ex Quay (Duty Paid), at a named port -- the seller fulfills his obligation when the goods have been made available to the buyer on the wharf at the named port of destination, cleared for importation. The seller has to bear all risks and costs including duties, taxes, and other charges of delivering the goods to the quay. The seller is obligated to obtain the import license, either directly or indirectly. Only used for sea or inland waterway transport.

DDP
Delivered Duty Paid -- the seller delivers the goods, with import duties paid, including inland transportation from import point to the buyer's premises.

DDU
Delivered Duty Unpaid -- only the transportation customs duty and taxes are paid by the consignee. From Dock - Seller owns goods until they are unloaded on dock at port of discharge; selling price includes all costs so far plus cost of unloading from vessel.

EXW

Ex Works at a named point of origin (e.g., ex factory, ex mill, ex warehouse). Under this term, the price quoted applies only at the point of origin and the seller agrees to place the goods at the disposal of the buyer at the specified place on the date or within the period fixed. All other charges are for the account of the buyer.

FAS

Free Alongside Ship, at a named U.S. port of export. Under this term, the seller quotes a price for the goods that includes charges for delivery of the goods alongside a vessel at the port. The seller handles the cost of unloading and wharfage; loading, ocean transportation, and insurance costs are left to the buyer.

FCA

Free Carrier, to a named place. This term replaces the former "FOB named inland port" to designate the seller's responsibility for the cost of loading goods at the named shipping point. It may be used for multimodal transport, container stations, and any mode of transport, including air. The seller is responsible for loading goods into the means of transportation; the buyer is responsible for all subsequent expenses. If a port of exportation is named, the costs of transporting the goods to the named port are included in the price.

FOB/FAS ENDORSEMENT

If a merchant sells on FOB, FAS, C&F or similar terms, it is the buyer's responsibility to place the insurance.

29 Trade Terms and Definitions

Students and Lecturers are advised that for the IIPMM Transport and Distribution examinations, knowledge and understanding of those terms marked *** is required.

Abandonment
A marine insurance term implying the "constructive total loss" of a vessel, and its transfer from the original owner to the under-writers.

Acceptance
A draft, payable at a fixed or determinable future date, upon the face of which has been acknowledged in writing the unconditional obligation of the person upon whom it is drawn to pay it at maturity.

(a) Bank Acceptance - a draft of which a bank is drawee and acceptor.

(b) Trade Acceptance - a draft of which the drawee and acceptor is a mercantile concern. Such an acceptance usually arises from the sale of merchandise.

***Accommodation Bill
A bill of exchange for which no value has been given, and for which no party is liable until such value is given. (Ref. Bill of Exchange)

***Accommodation Parties
Parties to an accommodation bill.

***Ad Valorem Duty
According to the value. An assessment of a certain rate per cent on the actual value of an article.

Advance Freight
Payment on account of freight to cover ship's outlay during loading.

Advice Note: A letter informing the recipient that a business transaction is being undertaken or completed on his behalf.

After Date
When a draft bears this phrase, the time begins to run from its date. The date of maturity is, therefore, fixed and does not depend upon presentation or acceptance.

After Sight
When a draft bears this phrase, the time begins to run from its presentation to its acceptance.

Trade Terms and Definitions (continued)

Agio
Premium paid for exchange of one currency for another.

***The Airwaybill - AWB
The Airwaybill is approximately equal to the Seafreight Bill of Lading. It is a form of consignment note used when goods are shipped by air. It also functions as a receipt and is evidence of a ***Contract of Carriage***. However, the *essential difference is that it is not a negotiable* title to the goods in the same way as the shipping Bill of Lading. It is widely used as a valuable receipt and as evidence of dispatch. It can, at times, be used within the framework of payment methods.
Note: On 1st June 1998 the 1975 (seventy-five) Montreal Protocol No 4 was ratified. This amended the Warsaw Convention of 1929, and now means that "paperless EDI systems " can be used.

Allonge: A slip of paper attached to a bill of exchange, acceptance, or note, for the purpose of providing space for additional endorsements.

Arbitrage
The buying of foreign exchange, securities, or commodities in one market and the simultaneous selling by telegraph in another market, in terms of a third market. By this manipulation a profit is made owing to the difference in the rates of exchange or in the price of the securities or commodities involved.

Arbitration of Exchange
Calculation of rates of exchange between two countries, but through an intermediate place to obtain more favourable rates. When two intermediate places are used it is known as "Compound Arbitration".
Average
A term in marine insurance signifying loss or damage to merchandise.

Back-to-back Credits
A term commonly used to denote letters of credit issued for account of different buyers to cover the same shipment, the terms of which credits are so similar that documents under one are subsequently applicable against the other.

B.F. Certificate: Issued by the Bureau of Animal Industry of the US Department of Agriculture certifying veterinary inspection.

Banker's Indemnity or Guarantee: A form required by the ship owner to be completed by the consignee, and countersigned by consignee's banker, when release of goods is required without production of the Bill of Lading. Also required when "clean" Bills of Lading are called for by Letter of Credit; and the shipowner, for various reasons, wishes to clause them.

Trade Terms and Definitions (continued)

Barratry
Loss caused by the wilful criminal action of a ship's master or crew.

***Barter
Exchange of commodities using the value of the merchandise as compensation instead of money. This scheme has been employed in recent years by countries having blocked currencies.

Bill of Entry
A shipper's detailed statement for Customs purposes of the nature and value of goods in a consignment.

***Bill of Exchange.
Legally defined as "an unconditional order in writing, addressed by one person to another, signed by the person giving it, requiring the person to whom it is addressed to pay on demand or at a fixed or determinable future time, a certain sum in money to or to the order of a specified person, or to bearer". It is the most general method of obtaining payment for goods shipped abroad.
(Ref. Accomodation Bill)

***Bill of Lading (Ocean)
A document signed by the captain, agents, or owners of a vessel, describing the kind and quantity of goods being shipped, the shipper, the consignee, the ports of loading and discharge and the carrying vessel. It serves as a document of title, a contract of carriage, and a receipt for goods

***CLEAN BILL OF LADING
A term used of a bill of lading when the transportation company has not noted irregularities in packing or general condition of all or any part of the shipment.

***STRAIGHT BILL OF LADING
A non-negotiable bill of lading in which the goods are consigned directly to a named consignee.

***THROUGH BILL OF LADING
A bill of lading used when several carriers are involved such as Rail Road, initially and then Vessel to final destination or vice versa. Used when transportation involves two or more connecting carriers. .
(An air waybill is essentially a through bill of lading used for air shipments.)

Trade Terms and Definitions (continued)

Bill of Sufferance: A coasting vessel's authorisation to carry goods in bond.

Binder: American equivalent of Irish "Cover Note".

Blank Endorsement
Signature on the back of a bill of lading or bill of exchange, without any qualifying instructions.

Blocked Exchange: Exchange that cannot be freely converted into other currencies.

Breaking Bulk: To open a consignment for the purpose of extracting samples or selling part.

Broken Stowage
Additional cargo which the charterer of a vessel must find to occupy space remaining available under a "full and complete cargo" clause.

***Cabotage
A point-to-point haulage operation within the territory of one State, by a haulier based in another State, (CITI). **(Important, refer to main text)**

Captain's Entry
A provisional entry passed by a ship's captain to enable him to discharge an entire cargo when this becomes necessary at a particular port, or when the merchant has failed to pass the bill of entry.

Cargo
Goods, merchandise or commodities of every description which may be carried aboard a vessel, in consideration of the freight charged; does not include provisions and stores for use on board.

***Carnet:
A customs document permitting the holder to carry or send merchandise temporarily into certain foreign countries for display, demonstration, or similar purposes without paying duties or posting bonds.

***Cash Against Documents
Full shipping documents are sent to a bank or an agent at the port of destination with instructions that they are to be handed over to the consignee only in exchange for the sum due.

***Goods (USA)
Cargo shipped by sea or air.

Certificate of Damage
Issued by dock companies in regard to goods unloaded or received in damaged condition.

Trade Terms and Definitions (continued)

***Certificate of Inspection
A document often required in connection with shipments of perishable goods, in which certification is made as to the good condition of the merchandise immediately prior to shipment.

***Certificate of Origin
A document to prove the place of growth, production, or manufacture, of goods specified thereon. The signature of the consul of the country of destination is sometimes required.
Countries which operate any kind of duty preferential system require a Certificate of Origin as proof that the goods qualify for preferential treatment. Commonwealth countries have a combined Certificate of value and Origin and this must be completed in duplicate and submitted to customs in the importing country with an invoice (see above). Other countries granting a Preference require a Certificate of Origin and this particular form is the one issued by the Chamber of Commerce.

Charges Forward
A banking term used when foreign and domestic bank commission charges, interest (if any) and government taxes in connection with the collection of a draft are for account of the drawee.
Charges to be paid by the buyer on arrival of the goods.

Charter Party
A contract, expressed in writing on a special form, between the owner of a vessel and the one (charterer) desiring to employ the vessel, setting forth the terms of the arrangement such as freight rate and ports involved in the trip contemplated.

Clean Draft
A draft to which no documents are attached.

Commercial Invoice
A trade invoice.

Commonwealth Preference
A system by which Customs duties are charged at lower rates than the standard rates, operating between the countries of the British Commonwealth.

***Consignee
The person, firm, or representative to whom a seller or shipper sends merchandise and who, upon presentation of the necessary documents, is recognised as owner of the merchandise for the purpose of the declaration and payment of customs duties. This term is also used as applying to one to whom goods are shipped, usually at the shipper's risk, when an outright sale has not been made.

***Consignment
A quantity of goods shipped (see also "On Consignment")

Trade Terms and Definitions (continued)

***Consignor: The seller or shipper of merchandise.

Consulage: Consul's fees

***Consular Documents
Bills of Lading, certificates of origin, or special forms of invoice, to which has been added the official signature of the consul of the country of destination.

***Consular Invoice
A detailed statement regarding the character of goods shipped, duly certified by the consul at the port of shipment and required by certain countries.
Consular Invoices are mandatory when shipping to certain countries, e.g. South America and the Philippines. These are specially printed documents which must be completed exactly in accordance with requirements and "visaed" (stamped by the Consulate of the importing country). The exporter must first buy a set of these invoice forms from the local Consulate; complete the documents according to the particular country's requirements and re-submit the set to the Consul for legislation.

Consular Visa: An official signature affixed to certain shipping documents by the consul of the country of destination.

Contract System: An alternative to the Deferred Rebate System: Shippers sign a contract in advance, either for yearly or indefinite periods, in which they undertake to confine all their shipments to Conference Lines' vessels.

***Cost and Freight (Incoterm: CFR. C&F still in use sometimes)
Same as C.I.F., *except* that insurance is covered by the buyer.

***Cost and Insurance: Same as C.I.F., *except* that freight is paid by the buyer.

***Cost, Insurance and Freight (Incoterm: CIF). A term used in connection with a price quotation under which the seller defrays all expenses involved in the delivery of merchandise on board the carrying steamer, and, in addition, prepays the freight and insures the goods to an agreed destination. The seller's risk terminates upon the issuance of Bills of Lading by the ocean transportation company.

***Counter Trade:
The sale of goods or services that are paid for in whole or in part by the transfer of goods or services from a foreign country

Cranage
Charges for use of wharf crane when ship's own appliances for loading are not used.

Trade Terms and Definitions (continued)

***Customs Declaration
Description of value and net weight of goods in a parcel sent by post to an overseas country.

Date Draft
A draft so drawn as to mature on a fixed date, irrespective of acceptance.

Deferred Rebate
A percentage of the net freight paid to the shipping company, which is returned to the shippers at stated periods to ensure their exclusive support of a particular shipping line or group of lines.

***Demurrage: Is the charge made for delays to barges, ships, etc., after a stated free period.

Disbursements
Shipper's charges collected by the ship owner from the consignee on the shipper's behalf.

Discount
(a) Commercial - An allowance from the quoted price of goods, made usually by the deduction of a certain percentage from the invoice price.
(b) Financial - A deduction from the face value of commercial paper, such as bills of exchange and acceptances, in consideration of receipt by the seller of cash before maturity date. The rates of discount vary according to the state of the given money market, the financial standing of the persons involved, and other circumstances surrounding the transaction.

***Dock Leveller
A movable ramp, (or a movable section of a ramp), which is used to make unloading of materials from vehicles of different tail-to-ground heights, safe and convenient.

Dock Receipt
Receipt issued by an ocean carrier or its agent for merchandise delivered at its dock or warehouse awaiting shipment.

Documentary Credit
A commercial letter of credit providing for payment by a bank to the named beneficiary, who is usually the seller of merchandise, against delivery of such documents as may be specified in the credit.

Documents Against Acceptance
Instructions given by a shipper to his bank that the documents attached to a draft for collection are deliverable to the drawee against his acceptance of the draft.

Trade Terms and Definitions (continued)

Documents Against Payment
Instructions given by a shipper to his bank that the documents attached to a draft for collection are deliverable to the drawee only against his payment of the draft.

Domicile: The place where a draft or acceptance is made payable.

***Draft: See Bill of Exchange.

***Dumping
Selling merchandise in another country at a price below the price at which the same merchandise is sold in the home market or selling such merchandise below the costs incurred in production and shipment.

***Dunnage: Are materials used for stowing and protecting cargo, or for protecting a vessel.
Silica gel - absorbs liquid eg Tarpaulin

***Duty Definition of Duty: *"A levy on imports paid to public revenue"*

(a) *Ad valorem* duty - According to value. An assessment at a certain rate per cent on the actual CIF value of an article. (CIF: cost, insurance, and freight).
(b) *Specified* duty - An assessment on the weight or quantity of an article without reference to its monetary value or market price.
(c) *Drawback* - A recovery in whole or in part of duty paid on imported merchandise at the time of re-exportation whether in the same or in a different form, i.e. as part of a manufactured material.

Endorsement
A signature on the back of a negotiable instrument made primarily for the purpose of transferring the rights of the holder to some other person. It is a contract between the holder and all parties to the instrument. Each endorser orders the prior parties to fulfil the contract to his endorsee and also agrees with the endorsee that, if they do not, he will.

***Errors and Omissions Excepted - Disclaimer
A phrase accompanying the shipper's signature on an invoice, by which he disclaims final responsibility for typographical errors or unintentional omissions.

Export List
The official list of headings under which goods for export are classified.

Ex-ship or Free Overboard
Sold free of ship, but not including lighterage.

Trade Terms and Definitions (continued)

***Ex-store or Ex-warehouse Sold form warehouse door, but not including cartage.

First of Exchange: First or principal copy of a bill of exchange to be presented and honoured, the other copies than being automatically cancelled.

***Force Majeure:
The title of a standard clause in marine contracts exempting the parties for non-fulfillment of their obligations as a result of conditions beyond their control, such as earthquakes, floods, or war.

Foreign Bill: A bill of exchange drawn on an acceptor overseas.

Foreign Exchange
A general term applied to transactions between countries involving the purchase and sale of currencies.

***Free Alongside (Vessel) (Incoterm: FAS)
A term used in connection with a price quotation under which the seller delivers merchandise free of charge to the steamer's side and pays lighterage expenses up to that point if necessary.

***Free Astray (An Air Freight term.)
A shipment miscarried or unloaded at the wrong station is billed and forwarded to the correct station, free of charges, because of being astray, hence, the term, free astray.

Free of Particular Average See Marine Insurance.

***Free on Board (Destination)
A term used in connection with a price quotation under which the seller pays all expenses and assumes all risks until actual delivery of the merchandise at the point agreed upon with the buyer.

***Free on Board (Named Point)
A term used in connection with a price quotation under which the seller undertakes at his risk and expense to load the goods on a carrier at a specified point. Expenses subsequent thereto are for account of the buyer.

***Free on Board (Vessel) (Incoterm: FOB)
Term used in connection with a price quotation under which the seller delivers the goods at his expense on board the steamer at the point named. Subsequent risks and expenses are for account of the buyer.

***Freight: *Payment* for carriage of goods or passengers, or for use of a ship.
The term is ***used incorrectly*** *by many to mean "goods" or "cargo".*

***Freight Account: The debit note received from the ship owner for freight due on goods shipped.

Trade Terms and Definitions (continued)

***Freight Forward: Paid by consignee.

***Freight Note: Ship owner's or broker's statement of amount of freight due.

***Freight Release
Ship owner's authorisation to captain to give delivery of goods, freight having been paid on them.

Future Exchange Contract
A contract, usually between a Bank and its customer, for the purchase or sale of Foreign Exchange at a fixed rate with delivery at a specified time. It is generally used because the customer is desirous of precluding the risk of fluctuations in the rates of Foreign Exchange which he may need at a future time or which may be due him at a future time.

General Average: See *Marine Insurance.*

Goods (USA)
Cargo shipped by sea or air.

***Gross Weight: Total weight of goods and packing. Total Nett plus Packaging
Nett = actual

***Health Certificate
In most countries, certain agricultural products, e.g. plants, seeds, shrubs, animals and animal by-products and foodstuffs must be accompanied by Health Certificates before importation is permitted. Some pharmaceuticals may also need one. A Health Certificate is issued by the Department of Health.

Home Value Declaration
A statement of value in country of origin at date of invoice. It is required from shippers in varying forms for those markets which charge their import duties on home values and not on replacement or CIF values.

***Hypothecate
To borrow from a bank part value of a consignment on the security of the shipping documents.
The bank has a "lien" on the goods and this is covered by a "letter of hypothecation".

***In Bond
Dutiable goods warehoused under Customs control pending the deferred payment of duties.

Trade Terms and Definitions (continued)

***Incoterms
See Part One - 25

Indent
An importer's instructions to a shipper or commission buyer to buy or supply and ship certain goods. If details as to brand, maker, etc., are included, it is a "Specific Indent"; if these matters are left to the shipper's discretion it is an "Open Indent".

***Inherent Vice
A condition causing damage to merchandise as a result of its own inherent defects.

***Insurance Certificate
A document in brief form issued by an insurance company usually to the order of a shipper under a marine policy and in cover of a particular shipment of merchandise in transit. Negotiability is effected by the shipper's endorsement and the title thereafter passes to the holder.

Keelage
Toll on vessels entering a port.

***Legal Weight
Weight of the goods and their immediate wrapper or container.

Letter of Credit - Commercial

A letter addressed by a bank, at the instance and responsibility of a buyer of merchandise, to a seller authorising him to draw drafts up to a stipulated amount under certain specified terms and undertaking conditionally to provide eventual payment for drafts thus drawn.

(a) Confirmed Irrevocable Letter of Credit - A letter to which has been added the responsibility of another bank, other than the issuing bank.
(b) Irrevocable Letter of Credit - A letter in which the issuing bank waives all right to cancel or in any way amend without consent of the beneficiary or seller.
(c) Revocable Letter of Credit - A letter in which the issuing bank reserves the right to cancel or amend such portion of the amount involved as has not been availed of, prior to the actual payment or negotiation of drafts drawn thereunder.
(d) Revolving Credit - A letter in which the issuing bank notifies a seller of merchandise that the amount involved when utilised will again become available, usually under the same terms and without issuance of another letter.

Trade Terms and Definitions (continued)

Letter of Credit - Commercial - continued

(e) Special Clauses -

1. Red Clause - A clause authorising the drawing of clean drafts (without documents) accompanied by a statement that pertaining shipping documents will be furnished later.

2. Telegraphic Transfer Clause - A clause containing an undertaking on the part of the issuing bank to pay the invoice amount to the order of the negotiating bank upon receipt of an authenticated cablegram from the latter that the required documents have been received by it and are being forwarded.

Letter of Credit - Traveller's or Circular

A letter addressed by a bank to its correspondent banks,authorising them to honour drafts of the holder up to the amount for which the credit is drawn. Such a credit is utilised to meet the expense of travel.

***Lien

This confers rights over certain goods, e.g. when money is borrowed on the security of a cargo the bank has the right to the cargo until the loan is repaid.

Lighter

A small vessel used to load and unload large ships

***Lighterage

The cost of loading or unloading a vessel by means of barges or lighters alongside.

Lloyd's Registry

An organisation maintained for the surveying and classing of ships so that insurance underwriters and others interested may know the quality and condition of the vessels offered for insurance or employment.

Loco: Covering cost of goods only, without carriage or warehouse charges.

Lump Freight: A single payment to cover the hire of a vessel.

***Marine Insurance Policy

A contract of indemnity by which an insurance company undertakes to refund to the assured the amount of loss arising from such marine casualty as may be insured against. Marine insurance is more extensive than other kinds, because it may provide not merely for losses arising from hire but from piracy, wreck, and generally all injuries sustained at sea.

Trade Terms and Definitions (continued)

Marine Insurance

(a) ***Average - A term in marine insurance signifying loss or damage to merchandise.

***(i) General Average - a loss arising out of voluntary sacrifice made of any part of a shipment or cargo to prevent loss of the whole and for the benefit of all persons at interest. The value of such a loss is apportioned not only among all the shippers, *including those whose property is lost*, but also to the vessel itself. Until the assessment is paid, a "lien" lies against the whole cargo.

(ii) Particular Average - a partial loss or damage of merchandise caused by peril insured against, but which is not a general average loss.

(iii) F.P.A. - Free of Particular Average - a provision in marine insurance policy that no claim shall be paid for damage to goods in the course of a voyage, unless a loss is sustained which is total or exceeds a certain percentage of the value as specified in the policy. The object of such a provision is the avoidance of petty claims.

(iv) W.P.A. - With Particular Average - Insurance against partial loss irrespective of percentage of such loss.

(b) Both to Blame Collision Clause - Protection against a disclaimer of liability appearing in some bills of lading when damage is the result of negligence on the part of the captains of both vessels that are parties to an accident.

(c) Casco Insurance - Marine insurance on the ship itself (hull) usually placed by the owners.

***(d) Cover Note - Temporary insurance coverage pending the later issuance of an insurance policy or certificate.

(e) Open Policy - A contract between an insurance company and a shipper by which all shipments made by the assured are automatically protected from the time the merchandise leaves the initial shipping point until delivery at destination.

Mate's Receipt
Receipt given for goods on being placed on a ship and pending preparation of bills of lading.

Trade Terms and Definitions (continued)

Maturity Date: The date upon which a draft or acceptance becomes due for payment.

Measurement Ton
For general cargo 40 cubic feet is a measurement ton and is regarded as being equal to 1 ton.

***Net Weight: Weight of the goods only, without any wrapper or container.

***On Consignment
A term used of merchandise shipped to an agent abroad when an actual purchase has not been made, but under an agreement by which the consignee is obligated to sell the goods for the account of the consignor.

On the Berth: Ready to load or discharge cargo.

***Open Policy
A cargo policy with no expiration date that provides automatic coverage of cargo to or from an assured in a specified trade at agreed rates, terms, and conditions. Usually consists of separate Marine and War policies.

Parcel Ticket
A receipt given by many shipping companies, in lieu of a Bill of Lading, for small parcels under a specified value, usually IR£5.

Particular Average: See Marine Insurance

Phytosanitary Inspection Certificate
A certificate, issued by the US Department of Agriculture to satisfy import regulations of other countries, indicating that a US shipment has been inspected and is free from harmful pests and plant diseases.

Porterage: Dock company's charge for porter's services.

Port Mark: The port of destination, stencilled on packages for export.

Primage: Ship owner's charge for use of ship's cargo-handling appliances.

***Pro Forma Sample - Not recognised so do not have to pay only Invoices which follows need be paid.
A Pro Forma Invoice - a specimen invoice. An invoice provided by a supplier prior to the shipment of merchandise, informing the buyer of the kinds and quantities of goods to be sent, their value, and important specifications such as weight, size, dimensions, etc.

Trade Terms and Definitions (continued)

Protest
A formal statement in writing by a notary that a negotiable instrument has been refused upon presentation for acceptance or payment and that all parties to the instrument, who are immediately notified, will be held responsible. If protest is not effected within the time fixed by law, the endorsers are discharged.

Quota
The quantity of goods of a specific kind that a country permits to be imported without restriction or imposition of additional duties.

Red Clause: See Letter of Credit.

Restrictive Endorsement
An endorsement on a bill of exchange which restricts the right of further transfer of ownership or specifies conditions for dealing with it.

Retire Bill: To pay the amount due under a bill of exchange.

Shipping Note
A memorandum addressed to the dock authority, which must accompany goods sent forward for shipment, setting forth the vessel's name and berth, full details of the goods and who is responsible for dock charges. Usually a standard printed form is used, in duplicate, the copy serving as a receipt for the goods.

***Ship's Manifest: Captain's statement giving details of ship, crew, cargo and ports of destination.

***Short Shipment, Shut Outs:
Goods not shipped by reason of arriving too late, the vessel being full, etc.

Sight Draft
A draft so drawn as to be payable upon presentation to the drawee or within a brief period thereafter known as days of grace.

Slinging: A charge for slinging cargo in chains ready to hoist on board ship.

***Specific Duty See Duty

Stowage Order: Before certain classes of goods, such as valuables, fragile or dangerous goods, are sent to the docks for shipment, a special stowage order must be obtained form the ship owner. It is the shipowner's authority to the ship-worker to accept the goods and stow them where indicated. It must accompany the goods to the docks.

Trade Terms and Definitions (continued)

Subrogation: The operation by which the insurance company, on payment of a claim, assumes all of the assured's rights to recovery from any third parties; substitution of one creditor for another

Surveyor : A marine specialist who examines damaged property and determines the cause, nature, and extent of damage and methods of repair and/or replacement. He is not an adjuster, and all his actions are without prejudice to policy terms and conditions.

***Tare: The actual weight of the container only, without the goods.

Tenor: The term fixed for payment of a draft.

Trust Receipt: An undertaking signed by a buyer, against which a bank releases merchandise to him for the purpose of manufacture or sale, but retains title thereto. The buyer obligates himself to maintain the identity of the goods or the proceeds thereof distinct from the rest of his assets and to hold them to repossession by the bank.

Usance: Period of currency of bills of exchange according to established custom in the market on which they are drawn.

Warehouse Receipt: A receipt given by a warehouse operative for goods received by him into storage.

(a) Negotiable - transferable by endorsement and requiring surrender of the receipt to the warehouseman to obtain delivery of the goods.

(b) Non-Negotiable - not transferable and undertaking to deliver the goods only to the person named therein or to a third party only on written order (delivery order).

***Weight

(a) ***Gross - generally, the total weight of the merchandise including all containers and packing material as shipped.

(b) ***Legal - generally, the weight of the merchandise itself plus the immediate container. This definition varies somewhat in different countries.

(c) ***Net - generally, the weight of the merchandise unpacked, exclusive of any containers. This definition varies somewhat in different countries.

Weight or Measurement (W/M)
Freight rates are often quoted W/M i.e. per 40 cubic feet or 1 ton, whichever works out greater.

Wharfage: Charge assessed by docks for the handling of incoming or outgoing ocean merchandise.

Wharfinger's Receipt: Acknowledgement of receipt of goods for shipment by a wharfinger.

No Need already covered

30 Part One Appendix 1

This appendix, which contains more detailed information than in the main text; is supplied to students for reference purposes only

Guide (only) to EU Regulation No. 3820/85 on Drivers' Hours and Rest Periods and EU Regulation No. 3821/85 on The Tachograph.

Introduction

This ***guide*** is intended to give a convenient outline of the principal provisions of EU Regulations No. 3920/85 on drivers' hours and rest periods and EU Regulation No. 3821/85 on the Tachograph and on the statutory instruments which implement these Regulations in this country. ***The information given is not exhaustive and is not intended to be an authoritative legal interpretation. Where necessary the EU Regulations and Statutory Instruments should be consulted.*** (Contact the Department of Public Enterprise, Dublin, 1.)

Definitions: In the EU Regulations, words and expressions have been defined as follows:

(a) "Carriage by road" means any journey, made on roads open to the public, of a vehicle, whether laden or not, used for the carriage of passengers or goods;

(b) "Vehicles" means *motor vehicles, tractors, trailers and semi-trailers*, defined as follows:

"*motor vehicle*": any mechanically self-propelled vehicle circulating on the road, other than a vehicle running on rails, and normally used for carrying passengers or goods.

"*tractor*": any mechanically self-propelled vehicle circulating on the road, other than a vehicle running on rails, and specially designed to pull, push or move trailers, semi-trailers, implements or machines.

"*trailer*": any vehicle designed to be coupled to a motor vehicle or a tractor.

"*semi-trailer*": a trailer without front axle coupled in such a way that a substantial part of its weight and of the weight of its load is borne by the tractor or motor vehicle.

(c) "Driver" means any person who drives the vehicle even for a short period, or who is carried in the vehicle in order to be available for driving if necessary.

(d) "Week" means the period between 00.00 hours on Monday and 24.00 hours on Sunday.

(e) "Rest" means any uninterrupted period of at least one hour during which the driver may freely dispose of his time.

Appendix 1 (continued)
Scope

In general the EU Regulations apply to carriage by road by:

(a) Goods Vehicles over 3.5 tons maximum permissible weight which in Irish law is deemed to be 1524 kilograms (1.5 Metric tonnes) unladen weight.

(b) Passenger Vehicles constructed and equipped to carry more than nine persons including the driver.
However,
(b)1. passenger vehicles on regular national passenger services where the route covered by the service in question exceeds 50 kilometres (31 miles) are exempted from use of the Tachograph but not from the drivers' hours requirements. In such an instance, a service timetable and a duty roster must be drawn up by the operator;
(b)2. since 1st January 1990, passenger vehicles on regular international passenger services whose route terminals are located within a distance of 50 kilometres as the crow flies from a frontier between two Member States and whose route length does not exceed 100 kilometres are exempted from use of the Tachograph but not from the drivers' hours requirements. A service timetable and duty roster must be drawn up by the operator;

The EU Regulations define *regular services* as services which provide for the carriage of passengers at specified intervals along specified routes, passengers being taken up and set down at predetermined stopping points.

Exemptions. There are three categories of exemptions from the Regulations:
A: Exemptions which apply to both national and international operations;
B: Exemptions which apply to certain national and cross-border operations,and
C: Exemptions which apply to national operations only.

A: Exemptions applying to national and international operations
1. Vehicles used for the carriage of goods where the maximum permissible weight of the vehicle, including any trailer or semi-trailer, does not exceed 3.5 tonnes.
2. Vehicles used for the carriage of passengers which, by virtue of their construction and equipment, are suitable for carrying not more than nine persons, including the driver, and are intended for that purpose.
3. Vehicles used for the carriage of passengers on regular services where the route covered by the service in question does not exceed 50 kilometres. (31 miles).
4. Vehicles with a maximum authorised speed not exceeding 30 kilometres per hour.
5. Vehicles used by or under the control of the armed services, civil defence, fire service, and forces responsible for maintaining public order.

Appendix 1 (continued)

A: Exemptions applying to national and international operations (continued)

6. Vehicles used in connection with the sewerage, flood protection, water, gas and electricity services, highway maintenance and control, refuse collection and disposal, telegraph and telephone services, carriage of postal articles, radio and television broadcasting and the detection of radio or television transmitters or receivers.
7. Vehicles used in emergencies or rescue operations.
8. Specialised vehicles used for medical purposes.
9. Vehicles transporting circus and fun-fair equipment.
10. Specialised breakdown vehicles.
11. Vehicles undergoing road tests for technical development, repair or maintenance purposes, and new or rebuilt vehicles which have not yet been put into service.
12. Vehicles used for non-commercial carriage of goods for personal use.
13. Vehicles used for milk collection from farms and the return to farms of milk containers or milk products intended for animal feed.

B: Exemptions applying to national and cross-border operations

1. Vehicles used for carrying passengers, which by virtue of their construction and equipment are suitable for carrying not more than 17 persons, including the driver, and are intended for that purpose.
2. Vehicles used by agricultural, horticultural, forestry or fishery undertakings for carrying goods within a 50 kilometre (31 mile approx.) radius of the place where the vehicle is normally based, including local administrative areas the centres of which are situated within the radius.
   A vehicle which is being used by a fishery undertaking on cross-border operations
   is not exempt unless it is being used (i) to carry live fish. (ii) to carry fish which has not been subjected to a process or treatment (other than freezing) from the place of landing to a place where it is to be subjected.
3. Vehicles used for carrying animal waste and carcasses not intended for human consumption.
4. Vehicles used for carrying live animals from farms to the local markets and vice versa or from markets to the local slaughter-houses.
5. Vehicles specially fitted for uses as (a) shops at local markets, (b) for door to door selling, (c) for mobile banking, exchange or savings transactions, (d) for worship, (e) for the lending of books, records or cassettes, and (f) for cultural events or exhibitions.
6. Vehicles used for the carriage of goods which have an unladen weight not exceeding 3048 kilograms, (3 Metric tonnes/1.5 tons), used for carrying material or equipment for the driver's use in the course of his work, within a 50 kilometre (31 mile approx.) radius of the place where the vehicle is normally based, provided that driving the vehicle does not constitute the driver's main activity.
7. Tractors used exclusively for agricultural and forestry work.

Appendix 1 (continued)
C: Exemptions applying to national operations only

1. Vehicles used by public authorities to provide public services which are not in competition with professional road hauliers.
2. Vehicles operating, exclusively, on islands not exceeding 2,300 square kilometres (888 square miles) in area, which are not linked to the rest of the national territory by a bridge, ford or tunnel open for use by motor vehicles.
3. Vehicles used for the carriage of goods which have an unladen weight not exceeding 1524 kilograms (1.5 Metric tonnes/3 tons) which are propelled by means of *gas produced on the vehicle* or by means of electricity.
4. Vehicles used for driving instruction with a view to obtaining a driving licence provided a vehicle so used or any trailer or semi-trailer drawn by it is not carrying out a journey in connection with the carriage of goods or passengers.

Driving Periods, Breaks and Rest Periods

A: Driving time without a break
The maximum period of driving without a break is 4.5 hours, after which a break of at least 45 minutes must be taken. This break may be replaced by breaks of at least 15 minutes each, distributed over the driving period or immediately after it in such a way that a cumulative break of at least 45 minutes has been taken after 4.5 hours driving. During a break the driver may not carry out any other work. However, waiting time and time not devoted to driving, spent in a vehicle in motion, a ferry or a train, will not be regarded as other work. The 4.5 hours relates to driving only and does not include other work.

B: Daily Driving Period
The daily driving period must not exceed 9 hours which may be extended twice in any one week to 10 hours. The definition of a daily driving period is the driving period between any two daily rest periods or between a daily rest period and a weekly rest period.

C: Fortnightly Driving
The total period of driving in any one fortnight must not exceed 90 hours.

Appendix 1 (continued)

D: Daily Rest: 1. In each period of 24 hours, the driver must have a daily rest of at least 11 consecutive hours which may be reduced to not less than 9 consecutive hours not more than 3 times in any one week. Any reduction in the daily rest must be made up before the end of the following week and must be added to another rest of at least 8 hours. This compensatory rest may be granted, at the driver's request, at the vehicle's parking place or driver's base.

2. However, on days when the daily rest period is not reduced, a driver is allowed to split the daily rest into two or three periods during the 24 hours, provided one of these periods is of at least 8 consecutive hours duration. When the daily rest period is split in this way, the minimum length of the daily rest must be increased to 12 hours.

3. The daily rest period can be split into two to accommodate a ferry crossing. One part must be taken on board the ferry. The other part must be taken on land either before or after the portion of the daily rest period on board the ferry. The period between the two portions of the daily rest period must be as short as possible and must not exceed one hour before embarkation or after disembarkation including customs formalities. The driver must have access to a bunk or couchette during both portions of the rest period. Where the daily rest period is split in this way, it must be increased by two hours to 13 hours.

4. Two Driver Situation: Where a vehicle is manned by at least two drivers, each driver must have a rest period of not less than 8 consecutive hours during each period of 30 hours.

5. The daily rest period may be taken in the vehicle provided it is fitted with a bunk and is stationary. Rest periods may not be taken on a moving vehicle.

E: Weekly Rest: 1. Weeks are defined as: from 00.00 hours Monday to 24.00 hours Sunday.

2. During each week, a daily rest period must be extended into a weekly rest period of 45 consecutive hours. This may be reduced to 36 consecutive hours if taken where the vehicle is normally based or where the driver is based or to a minimum of 24 consecutive hours if taken elsewhere. Each reduction in the weekly rest period must be compensated by an equivalent rest taken en bloc, before the end of the third week following the week in question, and must be attached to another rest period of at least 8 hours. The compensatory rest may be granted, at the driver's request, at the vehicle's parking place or driver's base.

3. A weekly rest period beginning in one week and continuing into the next can be attached to either week.

4. A weekly rest period must be taken after no more than six daily periods. The weekly rest period may be postponed until the sixth day if the total driving time over the six days does not exceed the maximum corresponding to six daily driving periods (56 hours).

5. In the case of the national and international carriage of passengers, other than of regular services, a weekly rest period may be postponed until after no more than twelve periods if the total driving time for the twelve days does not exceed the maximum corresponding to twelve daily driving periods. In this case the two weekly rest periods are taken together (i.e. 90 hours).

Emergencies

A driver may depart from the provisions of the Regulations on drivers' hours to enable him to reach a suitable stopping place to the extent necessary to ensure the safety of persons, of the vehicle or its load. The driver must indicate on his Tachograph chart or duty roster, the reason for, and nature of, the departure from the Regulation.

Bonuses

Payments, even in the form of bonuses or wage supplements, related to distances travelled and/or the amount of goods carried are not allowed unless they are of such a kind as not to endanger road safety.

Minimum Age

While the bulk of the Regulations deal with driver's hours and rest periods and records there are a number of provisions on the minimum age of drivers, driver's mates and conductors.

A: Drivers of Goods Vehicles

The minimum age for drivers of goods vehicles.

a) For vehicles having a permissible maximum weight of not more than 7.5 tonnes which in Irish law is deemed to have an unladen weight of 3,048 kilograms (3 Metric tonnes/1.5 tons) - 18 years.

b) For other vehicles: - 21 years, or 18 years, provided the persons concerned hold a driver's certificate of professional competence (CPC) in road transport.

The certificate of professional competence is a document awarded to a person on the completion of a training course covering several subjects from general vehicle maintenance to general transport administration.

Enquiries on the certificate should be addressed to FÁS, 27 Upper Baggot Street, Dublin 4.

Appendix 1 (continued)
B: Drivers of Passenger Vehicles

Drivers of passenger vehicles on journeys beyond a 50 kilometre (31 mile approx.) radius from the place where the vehicle is normally based must also meet one of the following conditions:

a) have at least one year's experience as a driver of goods vehicles with a permissible maximum weight exceeding 3.5 tons (1,524 kilograms) unladen weight;

b) have at least one year's experience as a driver of passenger vehicles on regular services not exceeding 50 kilometres (31 miles approx.);

c) hold a driver's Certificate of Professional Competence (CPC).

This provision does not apply to a person over 21 years who had been driving passenger vehicles for at least one year before 26th January 1979. Neither does it apply in respect of driving within Ireland to a person who had the appropriate licence before that date.

C: Driver's Mates and Conductors
The minimum age for driver's mates and conductors is 18 years.

Records

(a) Where a vehicle comes within the scope of EU Regulation No.3820/85 the driver must keep records of time spent driving, on other work, on breaks or on a rest period. Drivers assigned to a regular service must carry an extract from the duty roster and a copy of the service timetable. However, from 1 January 1990, drivers assigned to international regular services (other than special category) must use an EU type approved Tachograph, approved, calibrated and sealed at an approved workshop. Almost all other drivers must use the Tachograph.

(b) The issue, completion and keeping of records is the shared responsibility of *drivers and employers.*

Appendix 1 (continued)
Timetables and Duty Rosters

(a) In the case of:
- regular national passenger services,
- regular international passenger services whose route terminals are located within a distance of 50 kilometres, as the crow flies, from a frontier between two Member States and whose route length does not exceed 100 kilometres,

a duty roster and service timetable may be used instead of recording equipment. The employer is responsible for drawing up these.

(b) Each driver assigned to such services must carry an extract from the duty roster and copy of the service timetable.

(c) EU Regulation No.117/66 defines regular passenger services as "services which provide for the carriage of passengers at specific intervals along specified routes, passengers being taken up and set down at pre-determined stopping points". It is for the operator to decide if he operates a regular service.

(d) The duty roster must show in respect of each driver:
- name
- place where based
- schedule covering both the current week and the weeks immediately preceding and following that week (i.e. for three weeks in all).

The schedule must include:
- daily driving periods
- other work
- availability for work.

(e) The duty roster must be signed by the head of the undertaking or by a person authorised to represent him.

(f) There is no official format for these documents and operators are free to provide their own versions.

Appendix 1 (continued)
Tachograph

The Tachograph is a mechanical device used as a means of recording drivers' hours. Vehicle motion is recorded automatically on the Tachograph chart, and the kind of duty if any, (driving, other work, breaks/rest period) the driver is performing.

Calibration and Sealing of Tachograph Equipment

To comply with the law, Tachograph equipment must be calibrated and sealed at an approved workshop. An installation plaque must be affixed beside or in the Tachograph head, showing the name, address or trade name of the approved workshop, certain measurements relating to the calibration of the Tachograph and the date on which these measurements were made. Absence of an installation plaque renders the vehicle's owner or, where the vehicle is leased, the operator, liable to prosecution.

In the majority of cases in which new vehicles have Tachographs installed as original equipment, no installation plaque is fitted. In such cases the Tachograph equipment must be calibrated and sealed at an approved workshop before the vehicle is put into service.

The Tachograph must be checked every two years by an authorised Tachograph fitter or workshop. It must also be re-calibrated every six years, and a new installation plaque must be fitted. The inspection carried out under the vehicle roadworthiness test does not meet these requirements.

Forbairt (formerly Eolas), Glasnevin, Dublin 9 is the Government authority with responsibility for the approval of workshops to install, calibrate and seal Tachographs - this work can only be carried out at approved workshops. A list of approved workshops is available from the Department of Public Enterprise, Dublin 1.

Use of Equipment
The employer *and crew members* shall be responsible for seeing that the equipment functions correctly and that the seals remain intact. Any operations or interference resulting in falsified readings or recordings is prohibited.

Appendix 1 (continued)
Responsibilities of Employers
The Employer must:

1. Organise drivers' work in such a way that drivers are able to comply with the relevant provisions of Regulation (EU) No. 3820/85 and Regulation (EU) No. 3821/85;

2. Make periodic checks to ensure that the provisions of EU Regulation No. 3820/85 and EU Regulation No. 3821/85 have been complied with and take appropriate steps to prevent repetition of any infringements detected;

3. Ensure that the driver has a sufficient number of record sheets at all times, bearing in mind the fact that these sheets are personal in character, and the possible obligation to replace sheets which are damaged or have been taken by an authorised inspecting officer;

4. Ensure that the charts issued are of an approved model and are suitable for the instrument in the vehicle;

5. Keep the record sheets in good order for at least a year after their use and give copies to the drivers concerned who request them;

6. Produce or hand over the record sheets at the request of an authorised inspecting officer;

7. In the event of breakdown or faulty operation of the recording equipment, have it repaired by an approved fitter or workshop, as soon as circumstances permit.
   If the vehicle is unable to return to the premises within a period of one week, calculated from the day of the breakdown or of the discovery of defective operation, the repair must be carried out en route;

8. Comply with any request made verbally or in writing by an authorised officer for the purpose of checking compliance with the provisions of the EU and Irish Regulations.

Transport Operators and Employers must not:

(a) Cause or permit any person employed by them to contravene any provision of the EU or Irish Regulations.

(b) Make or cause or permit to be made an entry on a record sheet or an alteration to a record sheet which they know to be false.

(c) Interfere with the Tachograph in any way.

Appendix 1 (continued)

Responsibilities of drivers in regard to the use of equipment:

A: Drivers must:

Use the record sheets every day on which they are driving, starting from the moment on which they take over the vehicle.

Ensure that if there is more than one driver on board the vehicle, that

- the distance travelled by the vehicle
- the speed of the vehicle
- driving time

is recorded on the record sheet of the driver who is actually driving.

Ensure that the time recorded on the sheet agrees with the official time in the country of registration of the vehicle.

Enter the following information on each record sheet:

- on beginning to use the sheet - their surname and first name;
- the date and place where use of the sheet begins and the date and place where use of the sheet ends;
- the registration number of each vehicle to which they are assigned;
- The odometer reading at:
  (i) the start of the first journey recorded on the sheet;
  (ii) the end of the last journey recorded on the sheet.
- The odometer reading of the vehicle to which they were assigned and the reading of the vehicle
- to which they are to be assigned, in the event of a change of vehicle during the working day;
- the time of any change of vehicle.

Operate the switch mechanisms so that the following periods of time can be recorded separately and distinctly:

- driving time
- all other periods of work
- other periods of availability
- breaks and daily rest periods.

When, as a result of being away from the vehicle, they are unable to use the equipment fitted to the vehicle, ensure that the various periods of time related to all periods of work other than driving time, "other periods of availability" and breaks in work and daily rest periods are entered on the sheet either manually, by automatic recording or other means, legibly and cleanly. "Other periods of availability" refers to waiting time (i.e. the period during which drivers need remain at their posts only for the purpose of answering any calls to start or resume driving or to carry out other work), time spent beside the driver while the vehicle is in motion or time spent on a bunk while the vehicle is in motion.

Appendix 1 (continued)

Be able to produce the record sheet for the current week and in any case for the last day of the previous week on which they, drove when requested to do so by an authorised inspecting officer.

Return the record sheet to the employer for inspection and retention when practicable but in any event, not later than 21 says from completing it.

When the recording equipment is out of order or operating imperfectly, mark on the record sheet or sheets, or on a temporary sheet to be attached to the record sheet, all information for the various periods of time which is not recorded correctly by the equipment.

In case of damage to a sheet bearing recordings attach the damaged sheet to the spare sheet used to replace it.

Comply with any request made verbally or in writing by an authorised inspecting officer in order to check compliance with provisions of the Regulations.

B: Drivers Must Not:

- Use dirty or damaged records sheets and the record sheets must be adequately protected on this account.
- Withdraw the record sheet before the end of the daily working period unless its withdrawal is otherwise authorised.
- Use a record sheet to cover a period longer than that for which it is intended
- (usually 24 hours).
- Make or cause or permit to be made an entry on a record sheet or an alteration to a record sheet, which they know to be false.
- Interfere with the Tachograph in any way.

Enforcement

The following officers are empowered to enforce the requirements of legislation:

a) persons appointed by the Minister for Private Enterprise, (Transport Officers)

b) any officer of Customs and Excise

c) any member of the Gárda Síochána.

Part One Appendix 2

This appendix contains more detailed information than is contained in the main text.

A.D.R. Amendment Regulations 1986 - Application

These regulations apply to the conveyance of dangerous substances in connection with a trade or business. If the substances are for private use the Regulations do not apply. The Minister for Labour, at that time, gave certain exemptions under the regulations.
Section IV of the guide to the conveyance of Dangerous Substances by road gives details of the vehicle signs to be used under the A.D.R. requirements.

The information given here is not exhaustive and is not intended to be an authoritative legal interpretation.
When necessary the EU Regulations and Statutory Instruments should always be consulted.

Checklist of Duties of Consignors, Carriers and Drivers under the 1986 Regulations
Note: This checklist should be read in conjunction with the Regulations.

Duties of Consignor

- Determine whether the substance is a dangerous substance as declared in the Dangerous Substances (Part IV Declaration) Order, 1986.
- Check whether the substance may be accepted for conveyance (Reg.10(1)(a)).
- Check that the packaging is suitable and secure (Regs. 10(1)(b) to 10(1)(a)).
- Ensure that the proper danger labels are affixed to the packaging (Reg.10(1)(f)).
- Notify the consignee of date of dispatch and probable time of arrival (Reg.10(1)(g)).
- Prepare Certificate and give it to carrier or driver. (Reg.11).

Duties of Carrier

- Determine whether the substance is a dangerous substance as declared in the Dangerous Substances (Part IV Declaration) Order, 1986.

- Check whether the substance may be accepted for conveyance (Reg.4(a)).

- Ensure that the vehicle to be used is suitable (Reg.4(d), 11(4), and 12(a)).

- Ensure that packages are properly stowed and secured on the vehicle (Reg.4(c) and 12(a)).

- Obtain the Certificate from the Consignor (Reg.4(b)).

- Arrange the route to be followed in consultation with the Consignor (Reg.8).

- Provide a suitable fire resistant pocket or box on the vehicle for the Certificate (Reg.11(4)).

- Make provisions for parking of vehicles used for conveyors of dangerous substances (Reg.12).

- Instruct driver in writing (Reg.15).

- Appoint driver in writing (Reg.15).

- Ensure that driver appointed is reliable and has received adequate training and instruction (Reg.15/16.).

- Provide at least two suitable fire extinguishers on the vehicle (Reg.17).

- Provide a tool kit, scotch tape, two suitable portable amber warning lights, suitable personal protective equipment and, where necessary, suitable respiratory protective equipment (Reg.18).

- Fit the appropriate danger plates and labels on vehicle (Reg.19).

- Instruct driver on circumstances in which danger plates and labels must be removed (Reg.19).

- Provide a first-aid box on the vehicle (Reg.20).

Appendix 2 (continued)

- If there is an accident arrange for an examination of the load, its safe removal and cleaning of vehicle (Reg.21).

- He must not wear any clothing or footwear which could give rise to risk of ignition, fire or explosion of the load (Reg.6).

- He must not have any matches, lighters, lighted pipe, lighted cigar, lighted cigarette, open flame or any spark producing device in his possession (Reg.6).

- He must read the Certificate given to him by the Carrier or Consignor and sign it when he is satisfied that he understands its content (Reg.11(2)(d)).

- Place the Certificate in the place provided in the vehicle (Reg.11(4)).

- Ensure that the load is secure and that all access points are locked (Reg.12(a)).

- Park the vehicle in a safe place (Reg.12).

- He must not carry passengers except crew members (Reg.13).

- Ensure that any portable lights being carried or used are suitable if there is any danger of a flammable or explosive atmosphere being present (Reg.14).

- Ensure that he knows how to use fire extinguishers, warning signs, appliances or other equipment provided (Reg.16).

- Remove vehicle signs and labels when they are not required to be displayed (Reg.19).

- Notify Gárdaí or other appropriate authority in the event of an accident involving a dangerous substance (Reg.22).

- Ensure that all valves and manlids are closed before moving off and if leaving the vehicle that all access points are properly locked (Reg.22).

- Notify Carrier in the event of spillage or damage to packaging (Reg.22).

- Obey any instructions given to him by the Carrier or Consignor (Reg.22).

Part Two: Logistics Activities of Distribution

Distribution

Concept of Distribution

As a concept, *Distribution* is a system or network of channels, chosen by a manufacturer to enable his finished goods to be made available to the end user, in the market or markets of his choice.

PDM

Physical Distribution Management is the task of ensuring that the goods, or services, produced by an organization are transported from the place of production, or origination, to the point of consumption, as safely, efficiently, and as economically as possible. This involves keeping the total stock, transportation and storage costs as low as possible.

With today's technology "the world is truly our oyster", Global Distribution is a consideration for everyone.

Distribution - Introduction

In the **IIPMM** diploma-course subject "Transport & Distribution", the word "*Distribution*" is used to describe the transfer of a product or service from manufacturer to end user. "*Distribution*" is a Marketing term.
The Marketing Institute describes Marketing as "the way of doing business which starts with the customer. It involves a broad range of management skills from research and product design to advertising and promotion to *distribution* and sales."

31 The Buyer, Marketing, and Distribution

Buyers experience Marketing in two ways:

(1) *as a range of integrated activities, organized by their own company,both internally and externally, to further sales.*

(2) *by being on the receiving end of the marketing activities of their suppliers and potential suppliers.*

Buyers appreciate the advantages of quality products made by reliable suppliers, but these products must be readily available through an adequate *distribution* or *supply* network to be of satisfactory value.

Usually, end users are of two types; (1) individuals in the Consumer market or

(2) firms in the Industrial market

(a) "*Consumer Goods*" is the usual description given to finished products sold to the general public, like food and washing powder which have a short life, and longer life items (consumer durables), such as furniture, TVs, cars, and certain clothes.

(b) "*Industrial Goods or Materials*" is the description for, raw materials, maintenance items, consumables, and capital items sold directly to manufacturers.

It is the policy of *some* suppliers to sell through an agent or distributor only; particularly in the case of *international trade*. A local distributor in a foreign market can be a great help to an exporter. The use of his local market knowledge, and use of an existing channel network, can obviously save the exporter time and money in costly research. However, some buyers tend to look at a distributor in one of two ways; (1) as a costly middle-man, or

(2) as a costly middle-man!!!

Use of Distributors to reduce the Industrial Buyer's Cost of Storage and Supplier Base

In the past, buyers faced with making the decision to buy from a manufacturer or to buy from a distributor, often favoured direct contact with the manufacturer. Today, buyer emphasis is placed on the importance of reducing the *cost of storage* and on the methods to achieve this - including JIT deliveries.
This fact, plus another emphasis - that of *reducing the supplier base* - has resulted in buyers looking at distributors in an entirely different light

The Buyer and Distributors with multi-manufacturer representation

Today's buyer can appreciate the advantages of dealing with distributors who represent many manufacturers:

(a) Blanket negotiation on a number of different suppliers' products can take place. Multy products eg Gulbarts

(b) The buyer can encourage distributors to add extra items to their product offer list, to suit his or her needs.

(c) With distributor co-operation, inventory levels at the buyer's firm can be reduced.

(d) With fewer orders being placed, the buyer's *cost of ordering* will be reduced; as will costs attributed to Goods Inwards and Accounts Payable.

(e) A distributor can guarantee to carry stock to meet the buyer's requirements.

(f) Purchases can be covered by one annual "call-off" purchase order. In designing and using a routine ordering system for those 70% of purchases that only account for 10% of the annual spend, a buyer could effect cost reductions by dealing with a few distributors, rather than many suppliers.

32 Channels of Distribution

A *channel of distribution* is the route or path a product takes from manufacturer to end user.

Some manufacturers sell to the end user through Wholesalers or Agents.
Others, industrial manufacturers, sell directly to their customers who are also the end users. This *channel of distribution* - manufacturer to end user - is seldom used at present for Consumer Goods. *** Indications are that this will change in time, with greater use of "satellite TV-shopping" (especially "interactive home shopping" on DTV-digital TV); and the use of Internet facilities like those available for Industrial Goods in the US. A growing number of US Industrial buyers source materials on "IndustryNet" and on similar Internet facilities.

The Functions of a Distribution Channel may include all the following:

(1) Physical movement of goods - receipts, issues or dispatch
(2) Storage of goods while awaiting sale or transit.
(3) Transfer of title to the goods.
(4) Presentation of goods for final purchase.

Wholesalers, Agents, Retailers

Wholesalers take full title to goods which they buy in bulk from manufacturers. They then sell and deliver the goods, in convenient amounts to Retailers; supplying them in a suitable "product mix". They allow the Retailers a minimum of thirty days credit.
"Cash and Carry" wholesalers and Discount Warehouses are usually situated outside city centres. Retailers provide their own transport, collect their orders, are not given credit terms, but are charged less for their purchases.

Agents (occasionally called *Brokers*) have had a mixed role in Ireland.
Normally the role of an Agent is as follows:

(a) an Agent does not take title to the goods,
(b) does not handle the physical transfer of those goods to the end user,
(c) primarily acts to bring one of his "Principals" (Suppliers) and buyer together.

Overseas Agents usually stock, sell goods or services *and* invoice customers. Their principals give them a commission on *sales value, or sales volume*, as payment.

*** **Of course, there are exceptions:**
Fast food products go directly to customers; production, distribution, and consumption take place on the same premises. And where would we be without the "Avon" lady and "Tupperware" parties!
Not all industrial goods are distributed through a direct channel. A large percentage of engineering and electrical equipment reaches the industrial buyer by way of distributors or import agents.

Irish Agents - the Past

Some Irish Agents have provided services to their customers more akin to those of a Manufacturer or Wholesaler; e.g. holding of stocks, breaking bulk, and transport provision. It is difficult to draw a line of division between this type of Agent and a Wholesaler. At present, Irish agents visit individual supermarket outlets and take orders.

Irish Agents - the Future?

In July 1998, the withdrawal of the Proctor & Gamble agency from Allegro Limited, after 41 years; is regarded by some as the beginning of the end for Irish retail distribution agencies. Distributors need to re-examine their core competences, to see if continuing "to go it alone" is still a feasible option. Amalgamation with or without diversification must be considered. *

Retailers

Retailers offer advantages to both end users *and* manufacturers.

(1) For customers they carry out similar functions to wholesalers, albeit on a smaller scale.

(2) For manufacturers they can do the following:

(a) Act as a source of information between them and the end users. *(Two-way communication is essential to Marketing!)*

(b) Share part of special advertising costs with the producer.

(c) In times of strong competition and high demand for seasonal products e.g. Christmas, the Retailer can partly finance extra stock holding to maintain market share.

Types of Distribution Channels in Ireland - Direct and Indirect

Direct Distribution

(a) From Manufacturer directly to End User.

Indirect Distribution

(b) From Manufacturer to Retailers, and then to End User.

(c) From Manufacturer via Retailer's warehouse to Retail shop or supermarket, e.g. Tesco Distribution (formerly Power Imports Ltd.)

(d) From Manufacturer to Wholesaler, to Retailers and then to End User.

(e) From Manufacturer to large Wholesaler, to smaller Wholesalers, to Retailers, and then to End User.

(f) From Manufacturer to/via an Agent, to Wholesalers, to Retailers, to End User

(g) From Manufacturer to a Professional Distribution Company and then continuing into the distribution chain as **(b)**, **(c)**, or **(d)**, above.

(h) From Manufacturer to Agent, and then to Industrial User.

(i) From Manufacturer to Stockist, then, to either Industrial or Retail customer.

* **Ref to sundry articles by Des Crowley - The Sunday Business Post 26th July 1998**

Channel Strategy - Choice and Policy

Choice of Distribution Channel

The achievement of Marketing objectives depends to a large extent on *choosing the right distribution channel(s)*, as part of a strategic (long-term) plan.
Each channel option carries its individual costs and degree of risk for a manufacturer, who should evaluate the alternatives before making a decision. Choosing **(a)**, could be the best decision for making *maximum* profit but could be exposing the manufacturer to the *maximum* risk of bad debts from retailer liquidations.
Choosing **(g)**, might produce *minimum* profit but could eliminate the risk of *any* bad debts.

Policy

There are three types of *strategic distribution policy*
Intensive, Exclusive, and Selective.

- *Intensive policy*: By appointing the maximum number of channels to ensure that the manufacturer's product will be available to end users wherever they may be, and whenever they require it, (e.g. cigarettes).

- *Exclusive policy*: Giving ONE channel exclusive rights to distribute and sell the product. Sometimes there is an agreement made that the chosen channel will not sell products from the firm's competitors. *Individual firms must run a legal check to ensure that their version of "Exclusivity" does not "distort competition" as defined by EU legislation.*

- *A Selective policy* A limited version of the Exclusive policy, e.g. one retailer appointed for each town.

Types of International Distribution Channels

Sister Companies: The manufacturer sets-up a sister company, (i.e. a branch), in the end user's home territory, creating a direct link between the firm and the foreign customer.

Export Merchant: A wholesaler based in the manufacturer's country who buys goods and sells them abroad.

Overseas Agents: In foreign countries overseas agents act on behalf of the manufacturer. They stock and sell the goods and services of the firm, usually invoicing the local customers. They are given a commission on sales (volume or value), by the manufacturer as payment.

Buying Agencies: Foreign companies set-up agencies based in the EU, through which they can buy goods from European manufacturers and distributors. They arrange shipment to the destination(s) concerned.
EU companies can do likewise, of course, in overseas countries.

This type of distribution channel has advantages for both parties.

(1) The manufacturer is given a convenient method of exportation.
(2) A locally based agency will be aware of the integrity and reputation of locally based suppliers.

Distribution Channels and Standardization

Standardization is concerned with the concept of *Variety*. There is a natural tendency with Marketing and Sales departments to increase both the organization's "*product-mix*" and the *variety* of some products. Their intention being to cater for an additional market area, or perceived "special" customers.
The emotional argument put forward by Sales on these occasions with its declared "logic" of how the company must "go forward" can be amusing to the hardened stock-controller. Increasing product variety, increases both physical stocks, the cost of storing them, *and* can reduce transport load sizes. These costs eat into, or may completely consume the extra profit from these extra sales. The application of Pareto Analysis to product sales-turnover will, of course, show that a very large percentage of sales revenue is attributable to the sales of a relatively small number of product lines.

To prevent future obsolete stocks, throughout the *distribution* channel network, it is important for firms to maintain a *Variety Reduction* programme. This is simply a systematic periodic review of the current sales mix of products when their Stockturn and SVT (*sales value turnover*) are examined critically. Relevant de-listing can then take place. Accompanying this type of review can be a policy of: "*one old line out, before one new line in*", with Sales sharing the responsibility for obsolete stocks. The resulting "crisis of conscience" for Sales, encourages them to look much more critically at their "logical" suggestions in future.

33 Logistics and Physical Distribution Management (PDM)

Authors Dobler, Burt & Lee describe Logistics as the total of the activities of:
"Materials Management (MM)" plus "Physical Distribution Management (PDM)"

Where does Materials Management end, and Physical Distribution Management begin?

(a) MM incorporates the total flow of information and materials into the organization ending at the production line.

(b) PDM refers to the flow of information and materials from the production line to the end user. It supports the marketing concept of *customer service*.

The Primary and Secondary tasks of Physical Distribution Management (PDM)

PDM, being concerned with the detail of putting the *"Concept of Distribution"* into practice, does so as part of a Logistics strategic plan, (i.e. a long term plan to establish, develop, and maintain the organization's market presence). Marketing, Production, Stores, Stock Control, and other departments are engaged in different aspects of distribution.

The *primary task*, then, of PDM is the consideration, co-ordination, and integration of the *distribution responsibilities* of these departments; a task that makes necessary a proactive approach. (See "The Logistics Activity Mix)

Initial PDM decisions involve:

(1) Determination of customer Service Level; (*the number of orders available ex stock expressed as a percentage of the total orders received in the same period*).

(2) Agree appropriate Stock Levels to be held by the company.

The *secondary task* of PDM is one of ensuring that the finished goods or services produced by the organization are transported from the *Production point* to the *Consumption point*, as efficiently, and as economically as possible.

Fulfilling its tasks involves PDM in consideration of the following:

(1) Finished Goods.
(2) Packaging, (e.g. contents identification and ease of handling *in safety*).
(3) Warehousing.
(4) Inventory maintenance and setting of Service Levels.
(5) Sales Order processing, includes: convenience of placing order and advice on availability for the customer.
(6) Selection /Marshalling /Loading goods.
(7) Despatch, includes: suitability of documentation and reliability of delivery.
(8) Shipment Frequency.
(9) Movement and Transportation of goods.
(10) Customer Service, including point of sale support.
(11) Safety and Security issues.

Objectives of PDM

In executing its primary and secondary tasks, PDM sets out to ensure that all *distribution strategy* complies with:

1. The organization's Corporate plan.

2. Specific needs of the organization including targeted "Customer order-cycle time" * and choice of "Optimum transport mode" **.

3. Agreed customer Service Levels.

4. Agreed supplier or customer co-operation on relevant distribution factors such as, minimum order sizes, unit load types, delivery times and delivery vehicle size.
5. Minimizing total cost taking into account the cost of providing these Service Levels plus the cost of lost sales at each service level in the distribution chain.

6. Safe, efficient movement, and transport of goods.

7. Optimum utilization of distribution capacity.

8. Fast and accurate feedback of relevant information.

** Definition: "Customer order cycle time" is the elapsed time between the time a customer order, or service request is placed, and the time it is actually received by that customer. This can be a significant part of the lead time from the customer's point of view.*

*** Definition: "Optimum transport mode" refers to the task of choosing a mode or modes, e.g. Road, Air, or Sea to ensure safe, efficient, and economical movement of materials.*

Distribution and Elements of Customer Service

Often difficult to explain precisely, a working definition of *customer service* must refer to Distribution in particular and Marketing in general.
"*Customer Service is the customer's perceived degree of quality performance in a supplier's marketing and distribution activities.*"
Because most suppliers during the past twenty-five years, at least, have made quality a top priority, products of good quality have become or are becoming the norm in the market place. As a result, brand-loyalty in the market place, has decreased to a significant degree. Customer Service, from ease of ordering to after-sales backup, is often the single deciding factor in customer product choice.
The type of Customer Service provided by an organization, has always been related to that organization's marketing approach at a point in time. The evolution of Customer Service to the level of today's quality performance, is a reflection of the evolution of Marketing itself, a brief examination of which will be useful.

Of its nature, Marketing is energetic and dynamic. It has gone through a process of continuous change from the 1920s to the late 1990s. During this period it has been driven by either Production, Sales, a Market Concept or the current Market-Focused approach.

The marketing policies of the first half of the twentieth century began with: "if we can make it, let's sell it!" and ended with *"if others sell it, let us make it and sell it!"*

By 1957 the "Marketing Concept" had developed. This is an approach which:

(1) identifies the wants and needs of people in the market place
(2) verifies that the organization's product(s) can satisfy those wants or needs
(3) ensures a suitable *distribution* structure is in place for easy customer access to the product(s).
(4) ensure an adequate company profit can be made
(5) and then promotes awareness in the market place to points (3) and (4).

The early 1990s saw the development of the "market-focused "company, a term that suggests a narrower meaning than is the actual case.
Market-focusing involves not only "focusing" on and analysing the changing wants and needs of the market place, but also, "focusing" on and identifying the core competences (what we can do best) of one's own company. These unique competences are aligned with the wants or needs and opportunities of the market place to give the end user the best Customer Service possible.

Distribution and Elements of Customer Service (continued)

The elements of today's Customer Service do vary, of course, with the type of product and market concerned, but will include most of the following factors analysed under three headings:

Pre-transaction elements	*Transaction elements*	*Post-transaction*
Company Mission Statement Written Customer Service policy Order size restraints System flexibility Technical service	Ease of ordering EDI facilities Order cycle time Stock availability JIT facility Item substitution Order status information Order preparation Delivery time and Reliability	Complete delivery of order Condition of goods Invoice accuracy Customer complaints Claims procedure Packaging waste mgt.

Customer Order Cycle Time - OCT

Definition: Customer OCT is defined as "*the elapsed time between the time a customer order, or service request is placed, and the time it is actually received by the customer*." This can be a significant part of the lead time *from the customer's point of view.*

Elements of OCT

These are similar to a list of "True lead-time" elements prepared by a buyer.

- *Order transmittal time* — Usually the length of a fax call plus the time for confirmation
- *Stock availability.* — If stock is not available, a backup channel may be used.
- *Production time*
- *Order processing and assembly time*
- *Delivery time*
- *Customs clearance* — If supplier based outside the EU.
- *Quality Inspection time* — Does not apply to all materials, nor to some JIT or "Partnering" agreements

Distribution - Types of Demand - Where and When

Introduction

The nature of Demand determines how we control stocks. The levels of stock throughout a distribution network should reflect forecast demand. If a sales promotion is planned for three months hence, stocks in the various distribution channels will be increased.

Seasonal items like Christmas cakes or Easter eggs will have specific periods of demand.

Other seasonal items like Bathing Suits and Umbrellas will have a fluctuating demand.

(Umbrellas! *Fluctuating* demand in Ireland? Well, maybe not!!)

In general, the situation is not so clear-cut, so forecasting techniques are applied to past performance figures to arrive at an accurate as possible forecast.

Types of Demand - Dependent, Independent, Perpetual, Spike, Erratic, and Derived.

Demand is either "*Dependent*" or "*Independent*. "An item is said to have *Dependent Demand* when its requirement is directly dependent on its use in the production of a larger component.

An item is said to have *Independent demand*, when its demand is generated from many customers who buy only a small percentage of the total sales.

Perpetual Demand

Although demand for most products is governed by the Product Life Cycle, a life cycle of three to six years can be referred to as *Perpetual* Demand. This term also covers *Limited Time Horizon* products; products whose demand will conclude at a known future date greater than twelve months hence.

Spike Demand

Stocks that are held for seasonal items cannot be sold off without large percentage discounts. Orders are placed with little or no chance of return to the supplier, in the event of poor sales. These items are referred to as having *Spike* Demand patterns.

Erratic or Lumpy Demand

There are materials that have an overall Perpetual demand, which also have periods when demand is *very low* followed by periods of *very high* demand. The demand is unpredictable, unlike that for seasonal items. These items are referred to as having *Erratic* or *Lumpy* Demand.

Derived Demand

There is another category of items; those whose demand depends on the demand of another product(s). Labels for jams and marmalade, and packaging for paint, are two examples of items that are said to have a *Derived* Demand.

The controller of stocks for the distribution network must know *Where* and *When* demand volume will take place. By examining the sales forecast for retailers, the controller can work backwards through the channel network to set stock levels in each channel.

34 Selecting a Distribution System - Marketing Procedures

Having adequately researched a market to identify the needs and required benefits of current, past, and potential customers, Marketing will critically examine the ability of the organization to produce a suitable product, or provide a suitable service. Then, on being assured that the organization *can* do so, while making an acceptable profit; Marketing (by appropriate promotional activity) will try to persuade the market that the organization can satisfy their needs, both in product and in *availability* of that product. This is why choice of *distribution system* is so important.

The 10 Ds of system selection - areas requiring careful investigation

(1) Decisions. Examine alternatives, with reference to Marketing's customer knowledge. Who is the customer? Where is the customer? Where would the customer like to buy the product? What level of service does the customer want?

(2) Degree of Competition. Competitors' distribution systems and their nearness to the market have a direct bearing on their costs.

(3) Dedication. Faced with a choice of channel which also distributes other manufacturers' products, the question to be asked is: *"Are the type and volume of complementary or competitive items acceptable; or should a dedicated channel be sought?"*

(4) District Conditions. Unsuitable local conditions can adversely affect distribution of goods. Such conditions which vary from country to country and from region to region, can include climate and terrain, population, standard of education disposable income, government policies, social assistance and local transport.

(5) Distance. The cost of distribution increases with the distance travelled. More than one mode of transport may be involved.

(6) Demand from the Market. Bulk deliveries to a single destination are more efficient than separate deliveries to individual customers.

continued

(7) Density of the Goods. This involves the size-weight ratio, unique handling instructions, and choice of the most suitable transport mode.

(8) Development. Investment returns from a modified or new distribution system set up to cover additional markets, could prove disappointing. Restraint and care must be exercised.

(9) Data control. Will existing stock recording systems be adequate to provide data for control and distribution of stock in the proposed distribution network; or will changes need to be made?

(10) Difficulty. It is advisable to engage the services of an International Freight Forwarder, when intending to export goods to foreign countries, or dispatch goods to other EU member states. Otherwise, difficulties can abound. Familiarity with shipping documents, export licences, currency-rates of exchange, and EU regulations, is essential for ease of international transportation.

The 5 Cs of Distribution Management

An efficient distribution manager will have five goals for his distribution channel, goals concerned with cost, control, coverage, character and continuity.

(1) Cost. Distribution cost can be defined as the difference between the factory gate price and the price which the customer ultimately pays.
There are in fact, two kinds of cost; the investment cost in *setting-up* the channel, and the *maintenance* cost. The maintenance cost covers the salaries and expenses (e.g. cars) of a sales force or commissions of middlemen.

(2) Control. Using its own sales force will give an organization near maximum control over its marketing activity. Contrast this with an organization appointing a professional distribution company as a channel; a channel that has its own sales force promoting all the products it has on offer - not just those of the organization.
As an Irish firm's channel network grows longer, (*the "chain of distribution" in the home country or more especially, overseas*), that firm's ability to control price, sales volume, method and timing of promotional activity, and choice of retail outlets is greatly diminished.
However, there are some firms that are satisfied to place their products in the care of middlemen and leave destination control to them. This is often the case with many new firms just starting-up in business. They sub-contract as much as they can in the early years; production, warehousing, credit control and *distribution*.
There is a certain confidence for the end user in having access to the manufacturer. Where there is a long "*chain of distribution*" customers are, and can feel very remote from the manufacturer who is "untouchable." Recognizing this, in 1995, the Korean car manufacturer Daewoo began setting up their own mainland European and UK distribution system. Each dealership and sales outlet is owned by them, staffed by their employees who are paid by full salary, not by commission. Daewoo's second-hand car operation used this same concept. Customers feel they will not be pressurised into a sale. The manufacturer has *full channel control*; and customers know they have direct access to the manufacturer should a problem arise in future, or when advice is required. * The traditional dealership approach is the one considered for Ireland since January 1999.

***Coventry Evening Telegraph, 5th April 1996 pg 64.**

continued

(3) Coverage. The Physical Distribution Manager is concerned with two types of cover:

(a) the adequate geographical coverage of the market, to achieve the desired market penetration, and

(b) full coverage of the company's product range.

(4) Character. Marketing's job is to ensure that the character of the organization's product will meet the character of the market. To send frozen hamburgers to India, or to set-up a Mercedes-Benz dealership in a region of high unemployment where people could not afford to buy a "Mini", are hardly examples of good Marketing skill in action!

Likewise, the choice of distribution channel must suit the nature and characteristics of both the company and the market.

In some circumstances, matching the two characters is not possible, and some companies will leave or not enter a chosen market rather than compromise on their standards.

(5) Continuity. "Continuity" *in the context of distribution*, refers to the intention of Marketing to satisfy and keep their customers. Although. channel members would have been encouraged and *motivated* from the start by Marketing, it is still a fact that there is little or no sentiment in business. Most middlemen and retailers have little loyalty to their suppliers. They handle products while they sell well or give a good return. At some future time, there may be more profit for them in buying from a competitor. They may make a sudden change before the incumbent supplier has had a chance to discuss the situation with them. This is more likely to happen if the supplying firm does not have its own sales force. Where there is continuity, a channel is more likely to be consistent in giving good performance.

Costs of Distribution

Packaging and Packing materials.

(a) The longer the *chain of distribution* the more robust and expensive the packaging must be.
(b) The nature, or chemical structure, of the proposed contents may necessitate the manufacture of a package from expensive raw materials and closures, to ensure safety of personnel or/and convenient Handling, Storage, and Transportation.

Warehouse operation and maintenance.

Overheads, heating, lighting, labour, insurance costs.

Capital Investment

Cost of financing stocks to maintain agreed customer service levels.

Shipping.

Cost of despatch, materials handling equipment, documentation preparation.

Transport.

Cost of buying, leasing, or hiring vehicles, plus labour costs.
or alternatively, costs of sub-contracting.

Management costs.

Includes stores, inventory control, vehicle scheduling and routeing.

Damage.

Loss, damage or theft during storage or transportation.

Health & Safety issues.

Cost of complying with current or impending legislation.

Evaluation of a Physical Distribution System

A physical distribution system is composed of a number of channels. As part of the annual *marketing-planning* process, a set of agreed budgets and activities should be drawn up by the organization, for each channel.
At this *planning* stage the *control* procedures should also be designed and agreed. It will then be possible to measure variation from plan and identify the reason. The reason could be one or a combination of the following:

(a) the performance of the organization itself,

(b) the performance of the channel in question, or

(c) due to a change in the market.

Areas of Channel Performance to be Monitored

- Market coverage.
- Stock-outs and Substitutability. Will customers immediately select a competitor's product?
- Stock levels - were they adequate for suitable customer service?
- Despatch - accuracy and reliability of deliveries to the consignee.
- After-sales service and technical advice.
- Sales volume.
- Sales value after discounts, fees or allowances.
- Degree of face to face selling.
- Procedure(s) for handling "returns", repairs under warranty, faulty products, and issuing of documentation.
- Presentation of the product in store - *is it visible, attractively displayed, and accessible.*

On-going System Evaluation - questions to be asked

Is distribution network size, adequate for the size of the market?

Is the total cost of distribution and the cost per unit transported, within budget?

Are customers satisfied with the total delivery period from the factory?

Over a given period, what is the number of "stock-outs" per item, at the warehouse?

What percentage of the set customer service levels is actually being achieved?

What level of stock is actually needed at the warehouse?

Is there a computerised stock control system installed?

What is the rate of stock loss, due to damage or theft in the warehouse?

Is the materials-handling system in use compatible with those of the organisation and its customers?

Is the System dynamic, yet flexible enough to be easily modified, if circumstances change in future; e.g. taking into account the Product Life Cycle (PLC) concept?
Would the firm's toughest competitor give more satisfactory answers to these ten questions??? That is the most important question of all!

Distribution and Product Life Cycle - PLC

The author R.Bennett in the M+E handbook "Management" compares products to living organisms. "They are conceived and born, they mature, decline and eventually die."

Most products pass through a series of stages from the time they are introduced until the time they are de-listed from the firm's product-mix. Understanding this "Life-Cycle" assists the preparation of a successful marketing plan. A marketing plan considers the "marketing mix" of four key elements; Product, Price, Promotion, and of course, Distribution or "Place" as it is usually called, enabling these four elements to be called, the "4Ps."

The Product Life Cycle - PLC, consists of six stages:

Pre-launch

This includes design and development activity before the product is put on the market. *It is the time for Feasibility studies and Break-Even Analysis.*
These having taken place; the product is launched.

Introduction and Growth

Introduction
Costs are high and sales are low in these early stages of marketing. *It is a time of few competitors so the selling price is relatively high.* It will be some time before break-even is reached.
Growth
Sales and profits rise rapidly. Sales are far more predictable. *It is a time of increased competition and vigorous advertizing, as conventional consumers buy the product and profits peak.* Production and stocks increase, prices soften.

Maturity

Sales continue to rise, but slowly. *It is a time for product re-vamping, customer loyalty reinforcing, and seeking out new market segments.* There is a mass market, profits level off, prices soften further. The product reaches its ceiling and *Decline* will soon begin.

continued

Saturation

It is a time of extra promotional activity taken against the remaining competition, to combat a slump in sales, and shrinking profits. The end of the mass market is close at hand. *Decline* has begun.

Decline

It is the time when the product has lost its appeal, and is becoming obsolete. Profits are at or near zero. The product will be de-listed - taken off the market - to avoid making losses.

Product Life Cycle

It is obvious from the above, that when planning the PDM Strategy, the concept of the PLC as laid out above, has to be taken into account. For five stages of the PLC, *Introduction* to *Decline*, there will be a different or modified strategy, so it is important that the PDM function is continually aware of the current PLC stage.

Distribution Strategies for PLC

Introduction

Essential at this stage are initial stock availability, a good information system allied to quick replenishment in response to demand. However, *caution* must be the order of the day in relation to stock holding quantities after the initial launch. Until the *sales-volume success* of the product is measured over a suitable length of time, (judged from early market research and above all, experience), less than economic batch sizes should be manufactured to top up to minimum stock holding quantities, thereby avoiding potential long term stock-build. Integrated Logistics eases the way to implement this philosophy.

Growth

Sales are far more predictable. Service and cost can be better balanced. Adequate, or near adequate, service levels for each channel in the distribution network, can now be prepared. Raw material *economic order quantities* can be placed, economic batch sizes made, and product sales volume can be assimilated into the rest of the product mix. However, a warning! Increased market share and market growth are not the same. Without suitable monitoring and control during this period, increased market growth could well mask inefficiencies in production and *distribution.*

Maturity

Sales drives take place to hold market share in the face of severe competition. A good *distribution* system is now of paramount importance.

Saturation

At this time the product has its widest distribution. Planned service levels need to be monitored regularly in response to reducing sales. Why ? New Competitors.

Decline

A small number of existing customers may need to be serviced for quite some time, to cover their transition stage to another product or other supplier. This is more likely in the case of industrial products than of consumer goods. The system of stock control and length of the distribution chain will usually need to be changed.

35 Distribution and the Rôle of Despatch

The term Despatch (Dispatch) is generally understood to mean the delivery of stock items to the firm's *customers* at a given destination. However, customers are both external and *internal*. An *internal* customer of Stores is *Production*.

Despatch involves the following:

(1) Preparation of documentation.
(2) Checking accuracy of documentation before and after delivery.
(3) Provision of technically approved equivalents, if the items required cannot be supplied.
(4) The Selection of stock items from their relevant bin-locations
(5) The Marshalling of those stock items (grouping them together, e.g. onto a pallet.)
(6) Outer packing of marshalled items. (re-cartoning, "polywrapping", or sometimes shrink-wrapping.)
(7) Loading the combined items into a container, onto a truck or other vehicle, to be used for their delivery.
(8) Transportation of goods to the point of destination.
(9) Recording control information, e.g. frequency of stock-outs of individual items.
(10) Recording frequency of "urgent" deliveries to certain customers.

Points of destination include the following:

(1) Suppliers - return of surplus or faulty raw materials for credit.
(2) Other departments in the company - *internal* customers; this type of despatch is normally called "Issuing Stock."
(3) Quality Inspection.
(4) International Freight Forwarders.
(5) Customers - *external*.

Types of items to be despatched:

(1) Finished Goods.
(2) Transfers of raw materials from stores to Production.
(3) Items for quality inspection.
(4) Returns to supplier.
(5) Repairs - if the company provides such a service.

Despatch Documentation

Most companies are changing or have changed from manual preparation to computer preparation of their sales and despatch documentation. Some basic documents used in despatch are given different names by different companies; we will use the more popular names.

A **Sales Order Form** is filled out by staff in the Sales Office or CSU - Customer Service Unit. Each form has an unique Ref. Number, and it provides space for the following details:

(a) Customer's name, address, and Purchase Order number.
(b) Date and Customer's Account Number.
(c) Description of the goods and quantities ordered.
(d) Special handling or delivery instructions.
(e) Product code or part numbers.
(f) Agreed price, in case of a tailor-made item.

The Sales Order Form can be one page of a four or five-page NCR set, with each page being of a different colour to identify that copy's purpose. The use of different colours saves the printing expense of putting different headings on each page.

The top copy is kept in the Sales or the CSU office as a **Customer's Order Record**.
Copies 2 and 3; the firm's **Despatch Docket (Note),** and customer's **Delivery Docket.**
Copy 2, is signed by the customer, comes back to the firm, and is used as a **POD,** (proof of delivery), *and* as a source of information for Stock Control and Invoicing.*
Copy 3, the **Delivery Docket** is kept by the customer.
Copy 4 is used as a **Packing Slip (Note)**, and is placed in a transparent envelope and attached to one of the cartons containing the customer's delivery. Copy 5, the **Audit Copy** is given to the Accounts Department who keep their copies in numerical order, purely for "auditing-trail" purposes and to enable them to check that all despatches have been invoiced.

Other Documentation used in Despatch

A **Manifest** or **Loading Sheet**, (a list of the customers' orders to be carried) is used by drivers to check loads *onto*, and to check loads *off* their vehicles.

An **Internal Transfer Note,** used when a firm moves finished goods or raw materials to a section or branch of the organization in a different part of the country.

* **INVOICING: In companies with an integrated computer system, most of these documents are produced on line. A clerk directly inputting a customer's new order into the system sets off the automatic printing of all the delivery documentation on the despatch office printer. Stock Control records are updated simultaneously. Later that day, from the same information stored in the computer, the relevant Invoice can be printed off in the accounts department.**

continued

A **Return to Supplier Form** is used when goods or raw materials need to be sent back to a supplier for one of the following reasons:

(1) Damage to goods or excessive damage to packaging.

(2) Material has become obsolescent or obsolete, and is returned for credit.

(3) Sale or Return system e.g. paperbacks or greeting cards.

(4) Faulty material.

In the case of (1) or (2) above, a copy of a "Vendor Corrective Action Request" (VCAR) form, raised by Quality Inspection may be used if appropriately designed and agreed by QI, Purchasing, and Stores Management.

Sample of a VCAR form follows:

Seán Mac Gabhann Engineering plc

VCAR No	Date
00123456	4/1/2000

Vendor Corrective Action Request

Quality Improvement Process

Vendor Name:____________________ Part #:__________________

Description______________________ Qty.:___________________

GRN #__________________________ Location________________

Material has been received at our Camacside facility under the above P/O # and Corrective Action is now required.

Similar defects previously reported on VCAR #s______________________

(1) Description of defect(s)

Compiled by :________________ For QD ref:_____________________________

(2) For Vendor use only

(A) Do you agree with the defect(s) ? Yes/No

If No, why not?

(B) Proposed Corrective Action:

(C) Effective date of Corrective Action: / /

Name:_____________________ Authority____________________________

(3) Disposition of discrepant material: Defect Class ref #______

Compiled by:___________________ Authority__________________

For Quality Dept. use only

Vendor comments acceptable Yes/No_________________Specify if No

Name:____________________________ Date____________________

Vendor, please send response to +353 161 302098________Section________________

Sample of a VCAR form Sept 1998

The Aims of a Despatch Department

(1) The Primary and basic aim of Despatch is to service PDM adequately. This involves drafting relevant department policies and procedures, and by their systematic *implementation and maintenance*, to contribute to the overall profitability of the organisation.

(2) The Secondary aims follow from the first, and cover the *timely* drafting of strategic, tactical, and operational plans for the department. During the planning stage, is the best time to design the *control* procedures, an *essential* part of any planning process.

(3) Supplementary aims cover those necessary activities to be performed on time, and specific reports to be prepared on time, to ensure adequate management of the department.

Typical activities and reports would include the following:

3.1 The setting-up of a transport plan, to use maximum vehicle capacity, for journeys to customers

3.2 Systematic checking to ensure that all goods scheduled for despatch *are loaded onto* the vehicles *and are delivered.*

3.3 Set-up a "*perpetual analysis of deliveries*" system and produce monthly reports on items delivered and items not delivered. Detail reasons why items were not delivered, e.g. human error, service level too low for increased demand, or poor Sales-forecasting.

The Use of Third-Party Service Providers

Successive Irish Governments have continually advised, asked, encouraged, persuaded, and almost threatened, Irish Industries to ***export*** their finished goods. The importance of exporting could not be overstated.
The Culliton Report (1992), highlighted the need to focus on European markets and to generate more products with a high value-added input. As a result, more firms have become export oriented.

The choice of a suitable *distribution system*, if vital for home markets, is of *paramount* importance for export markets. For over forty years, the use of sub-contracted Transport and Freight Forwarding companies, has been a viable and proven way of distribution for Irish manufacturers. Contract Distribution, Warehousing and Stock Control, shared or otherwise, is also available. However, it has been less common to use sub-contracted Warehousing facilities, as a *permanent* arrangement.

Types of Third-party Distribution services

EDS An *Exclusive Distribution Service* is a service provided by a distribution company to one customer only. Marks and Spencer are served exclusively in the UK and Ireland by a number of providers including Transcare, and Fashionflow.

CDS A *Consortium Distribution Service* is a service provided by a distribution company to a small number of customers selling products to the *same* outlets e.g. newspapers to newsagents, and grocery products to retailers and supermarkets.

NDS A *National Distribution Service* is a nation-wide service provided by a distribution company having no limit on numbers of customers, or on types of products handled.

RDS A *Regional Distribution Service* is similar to the NDS, but covers a much smaller geographical area.

SPDS A *Specialist Distribution Service* is a service provided by a distribution company to facilitate the storage and movement of products; which of their nature require specialist attention, e.g. frozen food, hanging garments, china and glass.

NDDS A *Next Day Delivery Service* is a distribution service provided by a Courier for "specialist" items in small parcels, e.g. the Securicor service for Fiat and Ford motor parts.

SHDS A *Shared Distribution Service* is one where a manufacturer provides other firms with the opportunity of distributing their goods through his distribution network. Manufacturers would offer this service to optimise load capacity in their own distribution system; *but would be very selective in the firms chosen as "customers."*

Advantages accruing from the use of third-party service providers are important

Firms can shed themselves of the risks involved through lack of skills and "knowledge". Service providers can usually cover all risks by their acquired experience and knowledge, gained by having a broad customer base.

Improved resource management: capital tied up in vehicles is freed to be used in strategic areas. Firms can concentrate on their core business. In other words, "Stick with the Knitting" to quote Tom Peters. **(In Search of Excellence: Lessons from America's Best-Run Companies, Peters & Waterman, Harper & Row 1982)**

Firms can adapt and adjust to new or changing markets more easily.

Costs can be more easily identified and allocated to the correct market, or segment of a market.

When necessary, the service providers can be changed with little delay. However, *caution is advised in the drawing up of contracts*; as EU legislation can lead to claims for substantial compensation to be paid to existing channel member(s) if their provided service is cancelled by the firm.

36 Distribution Requirements Planning - (DRP), MRP and MRP II

DRP is a term that some students may not be familiar with, whereas they are probably familiar with, or are at least aware of, the terms MRP and MRP II.
Understanding MRP (MRP I) and MRP II should assist the student of Logistics to appreciate the concept of DRP; *but what is MRP and what is it all about?*
To simplify: MRP is concerned with the flow of materials and the precise timing of those flows to satisfy the requirements of Production. Thus, if a procedure can be developed by which materials required for manufacture are available ex stock, *at the times required,* and stocks of those materials at other times *are not kept*, or are maintained at a *far lower level;* an efficient purchasing and stock holding system can result.

MRP I, MRP II - Definitions

Materials Requirement Planning MRP (MRP I) is a system used in production and inventory planning with the intention of ensuring that the necessary raw materials (parts or components) are available at the right time and place, *and* in the correct amounts.
It starts with, and needs, *accurate forecasting* of the sales of finished products, resulting in an eventual Bill (list) of Raw Materials required, with the aim of ONLY holding stock to cover current forecast quantities. And, this stock is held in store, *only* when the suppliers cannot deliver the order "Just in Time.", i.e. as and when the materials are required.
MRP *does not* have to be a computerized system. However, computers enable "add-on" benefits which eventually lead to MRP II - *Manufacturing Resource Planning* - which is the expansion of the MRP concept to include the detailed planning of *all* resources required e.g. inventory levels, workforce levels, machine availability, "what if" options, and sometimes money.
DRP is the application of the MRP II concept to the management of finished goods and their effective flow through stores to the end user, by efficient transport support.

Distribution Requirements Planning - DRP - explained

Just as one aim of an MRP system is to avoid holding excess stocks at a point in time, the concept of DRP includes the elimination of unnecessary stock quantities of finished goods within the distribution system. The DRP concept is concerned with the accurate forecasting of demand for finished goods at the point of sale, and is compatible with the concept of MRP. Materials flow from their source of supply, through the network of channels and transportation modes, to the ultimate consumer. DRP systems endeavour to ensure that goods flow through the system on a time-phased basis and are available at the right channel at the right time.
Both DRP and MRP complement each other in the overall Logistics philosophy.

37 New Technology and Distribution

Without any doubt, innovative approaches, to the design of *materials handling and storage equipment,* improve customer order-cycle time. FLTs with on-board computers, and the use of Bar Coding save much time. It is however, ECT - electronic communication technology or "e-commerce" that is having a far greater impact on *Distribution* today, and will continue to do so beyond 2000.

EDI - Electronic Data Interchange is the transfer of data from one computer to another, (often without human intervention), via telephone lines. It is not a specific technology but a system of using existing technologies. These would include PC, Internet, bar-codes and telephone. Faster access speeds are possible by using special telephone lines developed to carry data - ISDN lines, (Integrated Services Digital Network).* ISDN allows simultaneous transmission of voice, text, data and images. Such is the rate of development in EDI technology that ISDN lines themselves may soon be superseded by systems that will provide even faster access speeds.

Because of the high cost in adopting new technologies, *telecom companies* are looking at ways to maximize their existing investment in infrastructure. DSL - Digital Subscriber Line - is a technology that has come as a blessing to them. DSL software enables larger amounts of data to be transmitted over *the ordinary telephone lines* than would otherwise be possible.

EDI Transactions. We are familiar with the improved "Query - response" EDI system used by travel and freight agencies in querying fares and available space, for air passengers and air cargo. Many similar types of transaction can take place by EDI, including *Production Scheduling, arranging Shipment Instructions, and the Transfer of Funds.* EDI systems enabling Irish buyers to check progress of every purchase order through all stages of manufacture and *distribution* became available in 1991. With prior agreement on the technical communication and message standards, computers at buyers' and sellers' premises can be programmed to talk to each other about *production plans, stock levels, material availability, and delivery times.*

As one would imagine, the Airline Industry was one of the early users of ECT for *Logistics activities.* The EDI standard for this industry, SPEC 2000, in operation since 1984, facilitates the exchange of *Materials Management* related information between Airlines and their Suppliers. Since 1993, AIRS (Airline Inventory Redistribution Systems) was integrated with SPEC 2000. EDI in improving content and speed of communication, shortens Lead Times.

Shorter Lead Times result in a range of benefits including the following:

(1) Reduced Stock Levels, (2) Reduced Cost of Holding Stock,

(3) Improved response time to customers' variable demand, (4) Improved Stockturn Ratio.

Other benefits from electronic communications include:

- *(a)* ***Lower administration costs***
- *(b)* ***Improved Cash-Flow resulting from easier tracking of outstanding moneys from debtors.***

New Technology and Distribution (continued)

EDI is described as a formal intimate computer relationship between any two users - e.g. buyer and seller. Buyers can solicit quotations, check material availability, place purchase orders, progress or expedite outstanding orders, receive consignment notes, and eventually receive invoices by an EDI system. Because invoices from different suppliers must have the same design and layout for EDI, a *Eurostandard* has been adopted. An EDI facility plus an organisation's own integrated computer network, can lead to an almost *paperless system* resulting in significant cost savings. **(See section on "Internet Security in Business" to follow.)**

Writing on *"EDI savings"*, author and Logistics consultant Matthew Walker says: **

> *"A comparative study of two blue-chip UK-based manufacturers, both of which sell similar products to the same customers, demonstrated the clear benefits (from EDI). One of the companies is an extensive user of EDI and renowned for its use of information technology. The other relies on the telephone and the postal service. The non-EDI user was found to spend twice as much on order processing as the EDI user. The EDI user could control stock levels more efficiently, and the rival was holding twice as much stock as the EDI user. In all, these differences accounted for a cost difference of nearly US$ 8 million per annum on distribution cost."*

In the US, President Clinton spearheaded the policy for *all government departments* to have computer systems installed to handle electronic documentation before 1998. Despite some delays, this policy was calculated to effect savings of US$ 3 billion.

EDI in reducing information transmission costs, is encouraging an increasing number of companies to examine the possibility of *global trading.*
An EDI link between buyer and supplier can be achieved directly, or via a "value added network" company called a VAN or a "provider". An Post agus Telecom Éireann set up subsidiary companies to act as providers, and in 1997 bought-over some existing companies as part of their strategic marketing rôle for the future. In 1993, the EDI sign up cost for multi-trader partners was a once-off fee of IR£ 6,500. Reflecting the drop in prices of computers themselves, EDI sign-up charges will continue to decrease in the immediate future. The actual usage charges are volume related. EDI messages can be sent over the Internet at a much lower cost, but with less security.

* **ISDN line facility was available to over 90% of businesses as at early October 1997, according to Telecom Éireann.; and should be available throughout the country by the middle of 1998. The use of ISDN for Internet access is growing rapidly in Europe,, from 4% in 1995 to 20% in 1996, and is expected to reach at least 45% by 2000."**
The Sunday Business Post - Computers in Business - 5th October 1997, and 19th July 1998

** **Article in "Logistics and Distribution Management" second edition. Edited by James Cooper.**
Publisher: Kogan Page Limited, London, N1 9 JN.

The Internet (www): is described as a "world-wide web of information machines". It is a global network owned by *no one*, which uses the TCP/IP protocol. By May 1999, it is estimated six and a half million computers connected to the network will be used by 165 million people.
Contrary to popular belief, the Internet is *not exactly a new phenomenon!* As part of the 1960's "cold-war" security programme, the US military and US universities combined their resources to develop a technology to enable different types of computers to "talk to each other" anywhere in the world *and to continue to do so if there is war.* Since then, universities, suppliers and companies that did business with the US military, found it useful to use this system, as did other companies that joined this expanding "INTERnational NETwork".
EDI can be called a formal system and the Internet can be called a casual system. However, with implementation of today's innovative approaches to security coding* and its current rate of development, the user's concern over its casual confidential nature may be set to end.

Internet-Security for Business
In the US, *encryption technology*, the process of scrambling a message at the sending stage and unscrambling it at the receiving stage, continues to produce improved standards of security. By order of the US Government, *the most advanced technology at a point in time*, must not be released to other countries. The US Administration is insisting on this to ensure, as far as possible, that the coding technology will not be used by international terrorists or criminals. Technology, *less than the most advanced,* may be released under a special licence.
In Europe, the route chosen by the EU Commission to solve Internet business security is to work with and alongside Irish company Baltimore Technologies, a world leader in cryptographic toolkits for electronic-commerce. They are located in the IFSC in Dublin, 1.

In Ireland the security of ***"E-mail"*** (electronic mail), which uses the Internet, (or an EDI linking system) was investigated by the Irish Revenue Commissioners. Because of the number of "hops" along the way in message transmission from sender to receiver, security cannot be guaranteed. In fact, the lack of security is quite surprising. Depending on the software used, certain pages of information can be protected by being made available to *"preferred viewers"* only. The Revenue Commissioners** *do not accept* this degree of data integrity for approved International transmission of invoices at present. Irish e-commerce businesses are subject to Irish tax laws.

Distributors and EDI transmission of Invoices
Distributors who have the facilities to use EDI transmission of invoices, may do so *by first obtaining written approval* from the office of the Revenue Commissioners. This approval, when granted to the distributor, covers only the Republic of Ireland. International transmission of invoices is not approved at present.
Not surprising, where taxes and VAT** are concerned, the Revenue Commissioners have employed highly qualified and experienced staff to examine all business aspects of IT and EDI.

EDI - "Fax-Bak"-E-mail

"Fax-Back" (fax-bak), is a development of basic fax technology whereby manufacturers and distributors, responding to questions received, are enabled to provide detailed information quickly for potential customers, without using up staff time. By using the Internet, however, manufacturers and distributors can provide a wider range of services to buyers, not just in some markets but in the whole global market. Catalogues of their products, with facilities to provide immediate answers on most quality or technical matters, can be made available to buyers using *"E-mail"/Internet.* As with other EDI systems, many activities from seeking quotations to eventual receipt of the supplier's invoice can be done by using "E-mail".

Connection to the Internet is made through one of a number of "Link" companies, again called VANs or ISPs (Internet Service Providers), as most are called nowadays. Examples are "EUnet", "Ireland on Line", "Indigo", "EsatNet", and "Telecom Éireann's "Telecom Internet". Cablelink plan to launch a *high speed Internet access* service by early 1999. While the number of connections to ISPs increases day by day as does the number of Irish companies using E-mail. Europe generally, falls behind the US in their use. The ISPs have different pricing structures with different permutations of set-up, E-mail address and annual fees. An average is not possible to calculate, but in mid 1998 intending "surfers" would have expected to pay up to IR£ 300 approx. in their first year for the basic service including four E-mail addresses. However, competition is the life of trade, and since "deregulation" other companies have entered the market in direct competition with Eircom (Telecom Éireann). In 1999 many of the new firms offer free internet access. Another cost is that of a high speed Modem, approx. IR£ 120, *if not included in the computer purchase package.* This is the device that enables computers to communicate with each other via telephone lines. Calls, including international calls, are charged at only the local rate between the caller and the link company, *so choose a link company with an access point near enough to allow minimum local call rates to apply to you.*

Another cost? After some weeks of joining the "club" you will be aware of the volume of time which Internet use takes. Soon you will have to consider another cost - installation charges for an additional phone line for dedicated Internet use.

***In July 1998, FIT - Fingerprint Identification Technology first became available in limited quantities in the US. This technology would replace "passwords" that can be stolen or forgotten. Registration of an individual's fingerprint is done by a tiny camera in the FIT reader. This converts the fingerprint image into a map of minute points, which is encrypted and stored in the computer or computer network.**
"The fingerprint cannot be re-created from the minute points" **the manufacturers wish to emphasise.**
"Retail organizations could be a major market area" **says Steve Torbe, product marketing manager, Compaq UK.**
(After article by Charles Hogan in The Sunday Business Post vol. 10 No. 35. 30th August 1998.

**** Electronic transmission of VAT invoices is covered in section 17 of the 1972 Act.**
This was up-dated by section 12 1 (a) in 1986. . This legislation was current as at September 1998.

Internet Costs - can be Low or High for a Distributor

Although relatively cheap for the facilities available, *intending users should carry out a detailed study* as costs for *their* type of use or *their* particular requirements could prove significant; e.g. the cost of setting up a professional looking web site. Having said all that, from a marketing point of view, compared to other forms of communications media, it *is possible* to set-up an Internet facility at a low and affordable cost.

World telecommunication companies are looking at the low cost per call situation with interest. There is well-documented information on the huge growth in computer sales for business and especially for the home. The percentage growth in US sales took a major jump when "*loan-leasing*" of computers was introduced by some PC manufacturers in the US, during the 1998 Summer. The main difference from other forms of leasing is that the customer *owns the PC from the outset* and can trade-up after every two-years. This removes the "fear of obsolescence".

It has been estimated that by the end of December, 1998, over a million people in Europe and sixteen million in the US will have an element of "CompuWorking" or "Teleworking" in their weekly schedule.* These future predictions of working from the home, together with the potential of the Internet being used as a new source of education and entertainment, will probably enable low call rates to be maintained, while telecommunication companies' profits rise. The Telecom Éireann, Ennis Town computer project is of interest in this regard. *Low call rates will encourage more and more distributors and small stockists to use this technology.*

On Friday 4th of September, 1998 US President Bill Clinton and an Taoiseach Bertie Ahern made a digital signing of a joint communiqué on e-commerce at Gateway 2000 in Dublin. It is believed that substantial reductions in Internet access charges will follow.**

Purchasing Cards and the Internet

Payment of invoices can be effected via the Internet. Modifications of an "electronic purse system" the "Clip Card" developed by Europay International launched in June 1996, continues to be used by IBM as an electronic commerce scheme." Manufacturers and Distributors accept transactions, via the consumer's Clip card.

The payment of Distributors or Manufacturers for small-value orders is a time consuming area of costly administration for buyer and seller alike. One way of overcoming this problem, using Purchasing Cards; is a method growing in popularity. Most of the banks in Ireland are expected to provide this facility by early 1999, as a matter of course. For those wishing to give their Purchasing Card numbers over the Internet, a security standard SET (Secure Electronic Transaction) was devised by the card associations together with the Netscape and Microsoft. Implemented in August 1996, two years later, it looks like becoming the standard.***

Internet Structure Stability

The Sunday Business Post, (5th October, 1997), quoting from a survey conducted by Dell, USA, says "the average wired household spends 12.8 hours per week "on line" compared to 6.5 hours per week twelve months ago." **** An estimate for 1999 is 15 hours per week.
During his Ireland visit in September 1998, US President Bill Clinton is quoted as saying that by the year 2000, one billion people are expected to be connected to the Internet by the year 2000.*****
All the use to which the Internet is being put, must pose a question in some minds, on the stability of the existing Internet structure. If the volume of current transactions increases and new Internet uses are designed, can the structure cope with the extra demand?
Delays accessing Internet Sites have already given a sarcastic meaning to www in the US: the "world wide wait". The many now engage in profitable "CyberTrade" or electronic commerce, together with the ISPs, will undoubtedly take the necessary action to protect the Internet, (or its successor), and secure their financial futures.

The Intranet is the private network version of the public Internet, used by companies for internal communications. It is used by many US organizations, to maintain document repositories for ISO 9000. Computerized Stores Vocabularies and Stores Manuals kept in this way, eliminate the risk of ISO inspectors finding *out-of-date* pages in one or more of the copy manuals used throughout the stores.

The Extranet is a communications system "between" the Intranet and the Internet. Unlike the Internet, the *Extranet* being limited to a number of designated users, *e.g. buyers, suppliers, distributors*, people are not slowed down by vast numbers wishing to access the same information at the same time. Suppliers' customers can access the Extranet to place, query or progress orders by password only. Security zones prevent unauthorised people from entering the system.

*** "The Sunday Business Post "-June 9th 1996 reported on a survey of Ireland's top 1000 companies which showed " ... that a majority already have the necessary technology to facilitate teleworking ... a quarter of those surveyed already allow their staff to telework, with the preferred arrangement being one day per week."**
The Forbairt publication "Enterprise Innovation", (July/Aug 1996, page 17), quoting from a Teleworking survey, stated that there were at that time, 15, 000 people in Ireland who teleworked regularly, and that this figure is expected to "more than treble" to 50,000 by the year 2006.
A Logistics and Social advantage of Teleworking is that the greater the numbers of employees that work from home, the freer will be the roads and highways for those who have no option and must travel to their work by road.
Refer to "The Sunday Business Post "-Computers in Business - page 4. 5th October 1997
(It is estimated now in September 1998, that there will be a further 300, 000 occasional teleworkers in operation, NMcI)
In October 1997, Hewlett-Packard in Ireland stated that 25% of their sales staff were currently working from home. Teleworking, enables employees to *"work smarter, not longer."*
For details refer to the Sunday Business Post - "Managing Your Business" section, page 14. 28th Sept. 1997

** **See the Irish Independent Business section 3rd September 1998**

*** **See the Sunday Business Post pg. 18 30th August 1998**

**** **After The Sunday business Post, 5th October 1997**

*****The Irish Independent - Business and Recruitment section 10th September 1998 pg 4.**

Digital Television - DTV

The concept of DTV - digital TV - visualises broadcasters providing interactive services to viewers of the type that the www does, with or without access to the Internet. By the end of 1998, Hong Kong Telecom will be in a position to evaluate their experimental IDTV (Interactive Digital Television) "home shopping" and "home banking" facilities vis-à-vis its advantages for business and the individual. Sky television in the UK is following suit in launching IDTV.
IDTV technology could case the strain on the www. Many satellite-TV companies are investing heavily in DTV with this in mind.

"E-commerce" Electronic commerce

Electronic Signatures Scan on-print signature Proof Thumb Print

Buying and selling products and services "on-line" is now usually referred to as "e-commerce". On Tuesday 2nd of September 1998 in one of the Government's newly adopted public/private partnership policies, the private sector was being asked to help fund the upgrading of the infrastructure for the Internet. This is part of a bid to make Ireland a *hub or clearing house* for "e-commerce".** The 4th September 1998 electronic commerce document digitally signed in Dublin by US President Bill Clinton and an Taoiseach Bertie Ahern demonstrated endorsement of Ireland as a future *hub* for US companies wishing to trade electronically with the EU and other European countries. There are thousands of jobs in relaying information across Europe.
As well as establishing an "e-commerce" industry in Ireland, global trading opportunities for Irish Manufacturers and Distributors will be a reality. European Internet and e-commerce market manager with UPS, Mr Martin Habiague believes that "e-commerce" will be a boon to the Transportation business".*

The Future

By 1983 Ireland had an excellent Telex system. Fax which had been introduced to Ireland two or three years earlier showed minimal sales growth. Buyers were waiting until all their suppliers had Fax machines and suppliers waited until all their customers got Fax machines. In 1986 with the arrival of improved technology and cheaper machines this stalemate was broken and sales of FAX machines increased ten-fold. Within three years Telex was almost a thing of the past. *** This change took 9 years to effect. Today major changes take less than 9 months to be implemented. Some buyers had been making it a precondition that their suppliers adopt an EDI system, and yet, E-mail over the Internet continues to grow in popularity. In 1999 45% of Irish buyers were using E-mail to a lessor or greater degree.
It is possible and quite likely that "E-mail" will replace "formal" EDI, just as fax did telex.

* **The Sunday Business Post - Computers in Business 6th September 1998.**

** **The Irish Independent - Business and Recruitment section 3rd September 1998 pg 3**

*** **(with the exception of many banking organisations, which appreciate its message traceability and security features)**

38 Y2K and Distribution

This chapter was written in August 1998. One thought then, that everyone would have taken the necessary steps to make their hardware and software year 2000 compliant, at the latest by the middle of 1999. Not so! One year later, people still needed to be warned by newspaper articles, and a government sponsored national poster campaign was deemed necessary. **(NMcI Oct 1999)**

Distribution, Stock-control and Y2K

By now almost everyone is aware of the so-called Y2K Bug or "Millennium Bomb". For many years now, the ability of many businesses to function has been dependent on computer hardware and software. This hardware, but more likely, this software, may experience failure when the new millennium starts on January, 1st 2000. The basic problem is not a virus or machine fault; it is a serious software oversight going back some 15 or 20 years.
At that time, presumably, the excitement of the new technology, the uses to which it could be put, and its huge added value to all aspects of business, were all that filled the mind of some software designers. As often happens in life, euphoria takes our mind off the basics in life, those fundamentals that are so essential to continued well being.
The design oversight seems so simple, it is hard to realise the tremendous implications it could have for each one of us.
Because we all use abbreviated numbers for a year, e.g. 14/12/56 for 14/12/1956 or 25/8/98 for 25/8/1998, software designers used this shortcut in their work to save disk space. Apparently no thought was given to the implications of using 1/1/00 for January, 1st 2000. Would computers read this as 1/1/2000 or 1/1/1900, or even something else? Dates may be rejected by the computer as incorrect data, lost data, miscalculated data or program failure.
Some organizations have planned to "con" their computers by changing the year 1999 to 1972 as the following year, 1973 had the same calendar as year 2000 will have.

Only a Date?

If it was only a date that was involved, that would be bad enough, but in spreadsheet programs the date is regularly built into formulae to make different calculations.
We will leave aside the problems for banks, building societies and insurance companies. Just look at one of the problems Y2K could cause for Stock-Control of a Distribution network.
The "cost of storage" of finished goods throughout the distribution chain is a matter for ongoing monitoring. Excess stock-holding leads to excess cost of storage which causes a direct drop in company profit. Software programs were designed to carryout all the required calculations enabling the stock-controller to have at any one time the information needed.
The cost of storage is expressed as a percentage per annum of the value of the average stock. The formula needs to calculate the number of months to which the percentage per annum will be applied. If the software reads 1900 and not 2000, the cost of storage will be calculated for more than 100 years, that is, *if the machine can take it.* Of course there is more than one type of problem with Y2K. Dates are also involved in more complex software applications.

What does the Y2K Bug actually do?

When the date changes from December, 31st 1999 to January, 1st 2000, the millennium Y2K Bug will come to life. The bug will affect the BIOS date that is stored as a sequence of numbers, representing Day, Month, Year and Century which will continue to read 20 and not 21, *unless the computer is year 2000 compliant.* DOS maintains its own copy of time and date information, but must get an initial value from the BIOS time/date or from its own program which stores the date as the number of days elapsed since January, 1st 1980. If the BIOS date is outside the range 1980 - 2099, DOS will ignore the BIOS date and start with its only known value usually January, 4th 1980.
The Y2K Bug can come to life when the computer is either switched on or switched off. If the machine is switched on, the first date of the year 2000 will appear as January, 1st 1900. If it is switched off, the date will appear as January, 4th 1980.
By the way, Y2K travels everywhere with the Wife! She is the Year 2000 Leap Year Bug. The year 2000 is a Leap Year because the number is evenly divisible by 4, but year 2000 non compliant machines will change the date from February 28th 2000 to March, 1st 2000, ignoring February, 29th. A computer will be unusable under these conditions.
Are we prepared for all this? In September 1998 it was estimated by the Chambers of Commerce in Ireland, that 48% of Irish businesses were failing to understand the problem or had not begun projects to deal with it. *
Overall Y2K awareness has been a high priority with IT professionals. The message began to get through to senior management shortly after the banks and finance houses issued information on their own structured millennium audit programme. Sufficient funding and resources are now being made available in companies to address this problem.
It is estimated that protection from the Y2K Bug will cost Irish businesses IR£ 7 billion.
However, the Irish Government are being asked by professional bodies to have Correction-Software regarded by the revenue Commissioners as a revenue item *and not as a capital item*, thereby reducing *profit-taxation* and improving the overall cost burden.

**[“‘My biggest worry’ said Gerry Condon, Y2K programme manager at the ESB, ‘Is that in January or February 2000 the directors of the company will turn around and say to us - you spent IR£12 million and nothing’s happened.’ He was joking, though perhaps not completely”]

2000 Compliance - Identification and Correction
The task is to examine machines and software for lack of compliance with year 2000. The entire supply chain and the software systems to support it will need to be tested for millennium compliance. Having identified the problems, they have to be corrected so that ***“neither performance nor functionality is affected by dates prior to, during and after the year 2000”**** The total cost of consultancy and resources to carryout an audit on this scale is very expensive. Most companies are finding it costing far more than their original estimate.”

The Task Continues As well as sorting out our own problems, we must encourage certain suppliers and customers to sort out theirs. *In helping them we are helping ourselves.* We can begin by preparing an ABC analysis of suppliers.

Classification of Suppliers

Suppliers can be sorted into three groups as follows;

"A" Those without whose raw materials or finished products we could not survive

"B" Those without whose materials we would be greatly inconvenienced, by buying elsewhere

"C" Those for whose raw materials we can buy technically approved equivalents elsewhere

It is a matter of priority then, to ensure that the "A" suppliers are taking steps to guarantee supplies to us without delays caused by late attention to Y2K.

Depending on the degree of integration in your distribution chain, a similar analysis can be carried out on customers.

Benefits of setting-up your Company Action Plan for 2000-Compliance

Externally

You will *keep* your customers by proving that you will be in business beyond 2000

Your business could *win customers* from less prepared competitors

Customers so impressed by you, will make you a *key supplier*

Internally

Despite the cost in terms of money and resources in carrying out a year 2000 compliance audit, it is a time when systems and system design can be re-visited and changes made to improve the core activities of the distribution business.

Effects of not setting-up a suitable Company Action plan for 2000-compliance

As if enough information is not known about the seriousness of the Y2K Bug to business, a good indication of the degree of seriousness of a given situation is the reaction of the Insurance Companies to that situation. The view of the insurance industry as expressed by the Insurance Federation is that Y2K computer failures are "*by nature both foreseeable and preventable*". This makes such failures a non-insurable risk and from September 1998 onwards insurance renewals included a lengthy disclaimer absolving the insurer from any liability for claims arising directly from computer failures caused by the Y2K Bug.

There are three unique features of the Y2K Millennium Bug.

Suddenness:	The Crisis will be experienced all at once. The symptoms are *fixed and sudden.*
All are effected	As with other bugs, Y2K is *no "respector" of persons.* Companies, large and small will be affected.
Critical	Companies can be put out of business *within hours.*
	Act Now

* **From a report in The Sunday Business Post 13th September 1998, on a survey carried out by the Chambers of Commerce in Ireland.**

** **From an rticle by John Dunne in The Sunday Business Post 19th October 1999**

*** **After the definition of the British standards Institute - BSI DISC PD-2000-1**

39 Implementing a Distribution System

Planning (which of necessity includes *forecasting*),
Directing (or leading others to accomplish a task).
Organizing, and
Controlling.

Planning is all about making *decisions*.
This requires the gathering of relevant *information*.
Information provides *alternatives* to choose from.
After evaluation of the good and bad points of *each* alternative, a *rational judgement* is made, and hopefully the optimum choice is made.

Plans are then moved from this decision stage to the *activity* stage of *Organization*.
By *monitoring* the results of these activities, comparing them to the original plan, *taking corrective action* where/if necessary, is how the essential management task of *Control* is exercised.
Applying this to *Distribution*, the early planning stage is carried out by Marketing in two phases:

(a) *Gathering information, and identifying "what the end user wants, and why?"*
Analysis of research information obtained from the targeted market(s), will indicate to Marketing the types of benefits which the people, living there, want from a specific product.

(b) *Gathering information, and identifying "how the end user wants to buy the product, where the end user wants to buy it, and what level of service, (pre and post sale), the end user requires?"*
Again, analysis of research information obtained from the targeted market(s), will present Marketing with details of products and services provided by competitors active in the area. A new entrant to the market(s) cannot give less service, or present a lower quality product and expect to survive in that market. The new entrant's product must be as easily available to, or more easily available to the end users. As part of the decision making process, competitors' distribution channels can be examined critically.
One of the suitable alternative channels available, may be the sharing of one used by a competitor.

40 Importance of Management Control - a final note

Having made the difficult choice of distribution network, the need for ongoing monitoring of the performance of the chosen channels is essential. The degree of *Control* that a manufacturer has over the chosen channels of distribution may be *total*, or severely *limited*. Whatever the degree of control is available, it should be exercised to the full, so that *early* corrective action can be taken when necessary.

REFER TO THE SECTIONS WHICH COVER
32 Channel Strategy, choice and policy
34 Selecting a Distribution System,
Costs of Distribution, etc.
35 Advantages accruing from using third-party service providers
33 Objectives of PDM and
34 Evaluation of a Physical distribution System

41 Student's Important Notes

Student's Important Notes

Student's Important Notes

INDEX

INDEX

INDEX

INDEX

INDEX

INDEX

INDEX

INDEX

INDEX

Chanel Tunnel advantages

1. reductions in cost due to a, speed, reduces travel time cost
b, Competition with Ferry Traffic reduced charges

2. Calais good dock facilities

Disadvantages

1. Have to still use Irish Sea ferry plus congested UK roads

2 A major tradegy could result eg fire

3, In time combustible materials and hazardous products may be restricted